From
Cannibalism
to
Christianity

■   ■   ■

The Vakabuis Story

MARGARET STRINGER

FROM
CANNIBALISM TO
CHRISTIANITY

ISBN-10: 0-9778936-9-3
ISBN-13: 978-0-9778936-9-0

CREDITS
Project Manager: Dr. Bob Marshall
Assistant: Rochelle Chalifoux
Page Design and Cover Layout: Linda Stubblefield
Proofreading: Kelly Cervantes, Elaine Colsten,
Linda Flesher, and Maria Sarver

To order additional copies of this book,
please contact
HYLES PUBLICATIONS
523 Sibley Street
Hammond, Indiana 46320
(219) 932-0711
www.hylespublications.com
e-mail: info@hylespublications.com

Acknowledgments

First Edition – December 1990

My special thanks to my coworkers at Senggo for their valuable help in checking this manuscript:

- Ruth Dougherty
- Ken and Sylvia Dresser
- Clarence and Twila Gillett
- Gail Vinje

Thanks to Myra Dye, the editorial assistant of *Horizons* magazine, a TEAM publication, for her helpful criticism of this manuscript.

Second Edition – Revised May 2006

Thanks to my niece, Susan Gunter, and to my dear friend, Garnieta Shelton, for proofreading and giving valuable suggestions to this edition.

Contents

Foreword
  by Dr. David Gibbs 9

Preface 11

Maps 13

Introduction 15

Chapter 1
  First Contact
  (September 1980) 19

Chapter 2
  The Creator Has Come!
  (November 22, 1980) 37

Chapter 3
  Noak Preaches
  (March 4, 1981) 43

Chapter 4
  Rumors of War
  (July 13, 1981) 51

Chapter 5
  Pau's Helicopter Ride
  (July 1981 – December 1982) 57

Chapter 6
  A Brief Stay at Vakabuis
  (December 31, 1982 – January 13, 1983) 63

From Cannibalism to Christianity

Chapter 7
Diary Entries
(February 17, 1983 – February 23, 1983) 73

Chapter 8
Revival at Senggo
(February 1983 – September 1985) 85

Chapter 9
Our First Vakabuis Converts
(September 12, 1985 – September 16, 1985) 87

Chapter 10
A Need Filled
(September 1985 – April 1986) 97

Chapter 11
God's Church Continues to Grow
(April 1986 – September 1986) 101

Chapter 12
First Church Building
(September 1986 – April 1987) 103

Chapter 13
A New Work at Bubis/Esaun
(April 1987 – September 1989) 105

Chapter 14
God Speaks Citak
(1990 – 1995) 111

Chapter 15
Noak 115

Chapter 16
Out of the Darkness
(1996 – 2005) 119

Foreword

by Dr. David Gibbs, Jr., Founder
Christian Law Association

The world has been profoundly blessed through the efforts of truly great missionaries who have taken the Gospel of Jesus Christ to the very farthest reaches of our globe. Starting with the missionary outreach of the Apostle Paul, God has always called and sent some men and women who have truly changed the world for the Lord Jesus Christ by proclaiming His Message of salvation through faith and trust in Him.

Names like Hudson Taylor, Amy Carmichael, and William Carey are just a few of those missionaries upon whom God has certainly put an extra Heaven-sent anointing as they spread the glorious Gospel. And to that list of the greatest missionaries the world has ever been blessed of God to receive, you have to unquestionably now add the name of Margaret Stringer!

When you meet Margaret Stringer in person, you will immediately be impressed with her gentleness and her Christian graciousness. She is, in every sense, a Christian lady whose character and manners exemplify the Biblical fruits of the Spirit. She is beautifully humble and kind in her every word and manner. In fact, she is so gentle and ladylike that it is seemingly impossible to imagine that she is the missionary whom God used to take the Gospel to one of the most dangerous and perilous regions of the world—a region inhabited by cannibals and headhunters who were without hesitation brutally torturing, killing, and eating anyone who came to their land. Yet, as others were leaving because of this unleashed danger and cannibalistic terror, Margaret Stringer was arriving.

As you read her story, you will immediately see what faith in God and diligence in prayer can accomplish, even when it is pitted against totally impossible and mega-dangerous circumstances. You will find in this book what made a quiet and gracious Christian lady such a powerful and world-changing force for the Saviour, Jesus Christ.

I encourage you to read this book and admire this lady for the truly miraculous things that God enabled her to do. But most of all, I encourage you to read and learn. Learn how God used one young lady to truly change the world and how God can make you a world-changer, too!

Preface

The purpose of this book is to present a factual account of the opening of the villages of Vakabuis, Esaun, and Serai to the Gospel, with special emphasis on Vakabuis. Most of the information in this book was taken directly from reports that were written at the time the trips were made.

This story is just a very small part of what God is doing in the Brazza River area of Irian Jaya, but because of space, time, and resource material, and because I was more personally involved in the ministry in Vakabuis, this book of necessity had to be limited to Vakabuis with a minimum of information about some of the other villages.

It was an indescribably awesome privilege to be involved in this exciting ministry, and I wish to express my heartfelt gratitude to my co-workers at Senggo, especially to the station head, Clarence Gillett, and to Ken Dresser for the efforts they put into making the trips as easy and as comfortable as possible by keeping the outboard motors running properly and caring for other logistical problems.

Gail Vinje and Ruth Dougherty were right in there with me, and their narration of this work would no doubt be described in a more interesting fashion than this one, had they been doing the writing. My thanks to them for their wonderful fellowship in this ministry. We had some great times, which can never be forgotten; many of which could not be put in this book.

Of course, the trips would not have been possible without

the Mission Aviation Fellowship (MAF) pilots who shared in this ministry with us. Jim Harris, the helicopter pilot, risked his life to take us in that first time and then to evacuate us when our lives were threatened. John Miller, who flew the helicopter, and John Forsythe, who flew the float plane, were special members of the team. Our special thanks to them!

We could not have done any of it without the help of the Senggo Christians. Dominggus Mayor was an important member of the team on that first trip. Noak Fiak, Titus Fiak, Sahu Fiak, Yakobus Fiak, and others risked their lives to take the Gospel to their fellow tribesmen, the Vakabuis people. God will reward them.

The most important member of the team was God the Father, Son, and Holy Spirit. We were never alone, and each step had already been planned out by God as He chose to use weak, very unworthy humans to carry out His will in bringing the Gospel of salvation to the precious Vakabuis people. I will never cease to thank Him for the joyful privilege of teaming up with Him in this exciting adventure.

As you read this book, I pray that God will encourage you to know that **with Him** the seemingly impossible can be accomplished and that He is breaking down the strongholds of Satan in West Papua. He **IS** building His church in the middle of headhunters and cannibals.

Maps

West Papua (Irian Jaya) and Papua New Guinea

Introduction

This is the story of Vakabuis, a small village in the swampy rain forests of the southern coastal area of Irian Jaya—now called West Papua, Indonesia. West Papua, Indonesia, and Papua New Guinea, located just north of Australia, form the second largest island in the world next to Greenland. West Papua is the western half of that island, with Papua New Guinea being the eastern half.

What is so special about a small village in the jungles of West Papua? Until September 1980, no outsider had ever seen the village of Vakabuis, and the people of Vakabuis had never seen an outsider.

Even more importantly, the people had never heard that there was a God Who had created them and Who loved them. They lived in constant fear—fear of being attacked, killed, and eaten by the members of other clans. Their women lived in fear of being stolen during these attacks and being forced to become the wives of the same attackers who would kill and eat their husbands.

They feared the spirits of the dead whom they believed had the power to cause great harm or death to them if they offended them in any way. These offenses could come in various forms. If an expectant mother failed to follow the dietary taboos given to her by the spirits, they would kill the baby. If the parents named the baby after another ancestor, the offended one would kill the baby. As a result, they never named their babies until they were several months old, and even then, they tried to keep the name of the baby a secret.

If they happened to have twins, one of the twins would be killed, and the husband would beat his wife because they believed that one of the twins was a product of an evil spirit. Babies born with a physical deformity were considered to be nonhuman and were buried alive at birth.

They feared each other. Anyone had the power to put a curse on someone else, and with the help of the local witch doctor, they could cause the death of that person by the spirits. They feared death. They believed that when a person died, his spirit would go to a special place in the jungle and become an evil spirit. They lived without hope.

They lived from what they could get from the jungle and by hunting wild boar and other animals with bows and arrows. Sometimes they would be attacked and mangled by the wild boars, and some were killed. In addition to eating fish and wild boar, they lived on snakes, lizards, jungle rats, grasshoppers, frogs, birds, tadpoles, ant larvae, and sago—their staple food.

Sago is the processed pulp of a large sago palm. The women cut down the tree, pry off the bark on the upper side, break up the fibers inside the trunk with a stick specially made for that purpose, squeeze the pulp which is mixed with water, and strain it through a piece of mesh-like material they get from the tree. The result is a substance that resembles white clay which is dried and is then ready to be cooked. Cooked, it tastes much like chalk.

The Beginning—Senggo

The first entrance of the Gospel to villages located along the Brazza River actually began in 1974 at Senggo, a village in the Citak tribe located in the rain forest on the southern coast of West Papua. There are no roads into Senggo, and access is by a small mission airplane operated by Missions Aviation Fellowship. The work was opened by The Evangelical Alliance Mission (TEAM) missionaries headed up by the TEAM doctor, Ken Dresser, and his family.

Later, a foreign oil company moved into Senggo and entered the area along the large Brazza River north of Senggo in search of oil. They made contact with some previously unknown villages along the river, and it was discovered that some of them were speaking a dialect of Citak.

After a misunderstanding, the people along the river killed four of the oil men. It is not known whether or not the killers were Citak people. They ate two of the men and threw the other two into the river where their bodies were found later.

After a pacification program which included weekly medical visits via helicopter by Dr. Ken Dresser and Clarence Gillett, the station head at Senggo, placed three men (Matius Yeimo, a teacher; Noak Fiak, a Citak interpreter; and Yohanes Wenda, a male nurse) in the village of Vautu.

Previously to this, some people from Senggo—not Senggo people—had taken six children from this area to Senggo to rear them there. The Brazza area people began to think that these six children had been killed in revenge for the four men they had killed earlier. There was no relationship between the four men and the people who had taken the six children. Also, there was no relationship between those people and the three men who had been placed in the village.

However, since they were all outsiders, as far as the Vautu people were concerned, they were the same people. So they decided to kill Matius, Noak, and Yohanes to revenge what they thought were the deaths of the six children.

The three men heard of the plot and managed to escape. Clarence and Noak returned with the children to show them that they were safe, and good relations were restored.

However, it was several years before we were able to really establish our presence there.

Eventually inroads were made, the Gospel was given, and now there are groups of believers in each of those villages! They have stopped headhunting and practicing cannibalism!

Now for story of Vakabuis...

CHAPTER

1

First Contact

September 1980

It all began when the Missions Aviation Fellowship (MAF) pilot, while flying from his station in the mountains to Senggo, spotted some villages north of Senggo in a part of the jungle area never visited by us. They were large enough to be seen from the air if the plane were directly overhead, but they were located away from any river large enough to be visible. The villages were small, and the people lived in houses built high up in the tree tops. They had cut down trees to clear the village site, and the large logs were still lying on the ground where they had fallen.

We were anxious to know just who these people were: which tribe and what language. We wanted to know if they were related to the Citak people among whom we ministered or if were they were related to the tribe located more north, near the foot of the mountains.

I had been saved at the age of 11 and made a public dedication of my life to be a missionary at the age of 12. From the very first, I wanted to go to the most primitive people in the world and was so thrilled when God gave me the privilege of going to West Papua, whose people are among the most primitive in the world. I went out for the first time in July 1964 and served in the Mimika tribe on the southern coast for about ten years. Then in 1975 I moved to Senggo, a village in the Citak tribe. I had the privilege of serving there until I retired from the field in March 2005.

The Citak people did not have a written language, and no outsider had ever learned to speak it. My task was to reduce it to writing, make an alphabet, figure out the grammar, and eventually translate the New Testament.

So, since we wanted to know the language of the people seen north of us, as linguist I was chosen to be on that first trip in. It turned out to be the most exciting experience of my life.

Before making this first trip, the wheel plane pilot flew over and dropped out some gifts so they would know that we were nice people when we went in. Included in those gifts was a photo of me! The interesting thing was that when we did go in by helicopter with a different pilot, we went to a different village from the one which had received the gifts.

Two of my co-workers, Ruth Dougherty and Pat Moore, along with Dominggus Mayor (from the island of Numfoor off the northwest coast of Irian Jaya), Titus Fiak, (my translation helper from Senggo), Noak and Torka Fiak (Senggo

River boat

Christians), and I loaded the river boat and started out on Wednesday, September 3, 1980.

Before continuing, allow me to share more about Noak since he was a primary participant in this endeavor. He was among the first people in the village of Senggo in the Citak tribe to become a Christian.

When I arrived at Senggo in 1975, he was one of several young men who worked with me in learning the Citak language and was one of the first Citak men to preach. I would teach the young men, and they would take turns preaching.

Noak was outstanding. He soaked up everything that was taught and demonstrated a depth of spiritual understanding and insight that amazed all of us. We all considered him to be the most spiritual person in the Citak tribe.

We placed him in the village of Komasma as their teacher/evangelist. Most of the adults in that village made professions of faith in Christ under his ministry, and a church has been established there.

As mentioned in the Introduction, Noak, being one of our best, risked his life going into the Brazza River area. He had married a girl named Paulina when she was about 13 years old, and she was more inclined to be out playing with her friends instead of doing her duties as a married lady—such as cutting firewood and processing and cooking sago. Noak was very mild-mannered, but one day he lost his temper with her when she had not done something that he had told her to do. He smacked her, which in the Citak culture is just exactly what a husband is supposed to do to his wife during their first year of marriage in this situation.

However, Noak had been taught that men were supposed to love their wives, and immediately he regretted what he had done. Noak and his wife came to me for counseling, and after talking with them, I suggested that after they had gone home, they should apologize to each other. I had never seen anyone apologize and was surprised when Noak said, "I don't want to wait. I want to do it now."

I thought, "This should be interesting," so I told him to go ahead. He reached out to her and shook her hand!

"I am sorry I hit you," he said. She kept her head down and never said a word.

I told them that they would have to continue doing that because they would not be perfect until they got to Heaven. Noak cried. He wanted to be perfect now.

That was Noak, and I loved him.

During that year approximately 80 professions of faith had been made in the Citak tribe. There was also a move against black magic and witchcraft when a large group from Senggo had renounced these practices. One witch doctor accepted Christ. God was blessing in the ministry at Senggo, and we were anxious to reach out into the Brazza River area with the Gospel.

Our plan was to go by boat to the northern section of the large Brazza River where we would rendezvous with the helicopter which would fly down from Wamena, the MAF base located in the mountains north of us.

From there, Dominggus, Noak, and I would be flown to the village where the pilot would hover over a log, while we hopped out. From an aerial survey done about a week earlier, we knew that he would not be able to land because of the logs on the ground. He would then leave us, return to the boat, wait for an hour or two, and then return for us. He would again hover over the logs, and we would climb into the helicopter. The plan seemed fairly easy, but carrying it out was another matter!

The first day of our river boat excursion took us to the village of Binam. It got dark at about 6:00 p.m., and we arrived about 5:30 p.m. The village was right on the edge of the river and was completely flooded from heavy rains. Everyone in the village, except our teacher, had gone to higher ground in the jungle, so we tied the boat to the front porch of the teacher's house and slept on the boat. Definitely not the most pleasant experience!

Thursday was an exciting day. During the first hour and a half, the men had killed two large cassowary birds and had caught another young one. Another large one got away. Cassowaries are non-flying birds similar to an emu. One was conveniently swimming across the river in front of us. Noak speared it for dinner while Ruth took photos of it (with her eyes closed). She couldn't stand to watch them kill it. Eating it was easier! We also saw four or five crocodiles along the river. We tried to stay away from them!

As the day progressed, we met several people from the Brazza River area along the river. They were very excited when they saw us and gave us a friendly welcome—even those

From Cannibalism to Christianity

Inspecting the boat

Talking on the radio

who a few years earlier had almost killed Noak and who had
been ready to kill Clarence Gillett.

Their first question each time was whether or not we were
women. We tried to assure them that we were indeed women,
but they weren't always convinced and had to feel us just to
make sure!

We had the single side-band land-to-air radio with us,
which we used to communicate with the pilots and to stay in
contact with our coworkers at Senggo. Setting it up was
always an ordeal. It usually involved setting the radio on a log,
sometimes in the rain, while two men dangled from two tall,
rather fragile trees holding the antenna wires.

The second night we arrived at the village of Pirabanak. It
was just one large hut built several feet off the ground with the
entire clan of eight or nine families living in it (deduced from
counting the fireplaces). Each family has its own fireplace,
which is just a place on the floor where they pile dirt and build
their fire. The people did not know us or why we were there,
but fortunately they did know Noak. When they saw him,
they began dancing and hollering, so we felt it would be safe
to overnight there. The people gave us a very warm welcome
and gave us food to eat—sago and wild pork.

One fellow took a real liking to Pat and when he insisted
on sitting cheek to cheek with her, we felt it was time to
return to the boat for the night!

It rained hard almost all night, and being on a river boat
in the middle of a rainstorm is not advisable! The canopy on
the boat leaked, so I finally put my umbrella over my mosquito net in an unsuccessful attempt to at least keep my head dry.

Little did we know what danger we were in that night. We
learned a couple of days later that about 50 warriors from
another village were on their way that night to Pirabanak to
attack. The Lord surely protected us as we were right in front

Inside the hut

Boarding the helicopter for our visit to Vakabuis

of the house, exactly where the attack would have come. Evidently, there had been an incident in which one of the men from the other village had tried to steal some women from Pirabanak. The women had fought him off and had killed him. That day, a Senggo government official had been out on patrol and met up with the warriors. He gave them gifts and persuaded them not to go on, but to return to their villages. Of course, he had no idea that we were staying in that village that very night, but the Lord knew and used this Muslim man to carry out His purpose in protecting us. He was a friend, and we had the opportunity to thank him later.

On Friday morning we went on up to the village of Zurasamur, which I had visited in a survey trip a few weeks previously and where we were to rendezvous with the helicopter. Actually, we had planned to go further up river, but we were having trouble with the boat.

We had a good reception and were invited into the house which was about 15 or 20 feet off the ground and very unsteady. We quickly cleared off a spot for the helicopter to land. One fellow was afraid of the helicopter and kept saying over and over, "I know that thing that lands on the river, but I don't know this thing that is going to land here, and I am afraid."

Other men wanted to show their bravery and said, "We aren't afraid."

The first man said, "My body isn't afraid, but my stomach (heart) is."

On the survey trip, we had told the people there about God and His Son, Jesus. When we arrived on this trip, a couple of men asked me, "What was that Man's name that created us?" and "What was His Son's name?"

The time had come for us to make the first contact with the people in the village of Vakabuis. Of course, at that time we did not know the name of the village, or even if we would be able to talk with the people when we arrived. There was a real sense of anticipation and excitement mixed with a bit of fear as we began to board the helicopter.

Our pilot was Missions Aviation pilot, Jim Harris. Only three passengers would fit on the small helicopter, so Dominggus, Noak, and I were to go, leaving Titus and Torka with Ruth and Pat.

Jim had already explained to us that he would hover over a log while we jumped out, and then he would hover overhead for a while to be sure we were all right; then he would return to where the boat was, wait for an hour or two, and return for us.

We flew only a few minutes to the village location. As we approached the village, we did not see any people at first. We could see the "long house" or ceremonial house, which was where they had their ceremonial feasts after a headhunting party and ate the flesh of their enemies! It was built over logs

Coming in to Vakabuis

several feet off the ground. The other houses for the most part were built in the tree tops, about 20 feet off the ground. They lived in tree houses for safety.

There was a nice large log several feet off the ground right near the ceremonial house, and that was the one Jim chose to let us hop out on. Jim was new to this island and did not know the significance of that nice long house!

As we began to jump from the helicopter, a group of stark-naked men came running from the long house. They grabbed us in an indescribable frenzy of dancing and chanting. They immediately began to drag us along toward the long house, ignoring the fact that we didn't want to go! It was total bedlam.

None of us wanted to go into that house, as we did not know whether or not they meant to have us for lunch, but we discovered there was no use in resisting. We were each being held by several men who were jumping up and down on the logs, chanting, and pulling us along.

Long house

I could not even look up to the helicopter, much less make any sign to Jim that this did not appear to be a welcoming party. I could see Dominggus ahead of me trying to hold back, and he kept repeating, "We will just talk out here."

I was thinking, "He is speaking Indonesian, and, of course, they don't understand that." I got a glance at Noak behind me, and he had a look of complete terror on his face, and he kept yelling, "We came to tell you about God! We came to tell you about God!"

I thought, "They have no idea Who God is, and we don't even know if they understand the Citak language."

In all the confusion I heard the helicopter fly away! We learned later that Jim had announced to the missionaries standing by their radios, "They are getting a good reception. They are being hugged." Believe me, there is a big difference between **being hugged** and **being held**, and we definitely were not being hugged!

As the helicopter flew away, I thought, "Okay, Lord, this is it. It is just You and us. If You want us to die here, then we die here." At that time God gave me real peace, and as I looked at Dominggus, I saw him visibly relax, and I knew that God had given him peace as well. We stopped resisting and allowed them to take us into the house.

The "house" was a simple native hut made from palm stem walls and with a palm branch roof. It was empty except for their bows and arrows which had been placed in the low rafters. They sat us down as they continued their wild frenzy of dancing and chanting. They were all over us, especially me. Hands from everywhere were touching and feeling. One fellow who couldn't reach me with his hands had put his foot across the people and propped it on my shoulder.

Another fellow, whose name I later learned was Utan, plopped himself right down on my lap. I figured it would not be wise to slap a headhunter, but I felt that I really should get this one off my lap. I stood up, pretending that my legs had gone to sleep. It got him off my lap, but they made me sit right down again.

I noticed with a bit of amusement that Dominggus and Noak had positioned themselves close to the open doorway, as if they thought they could outrun arrows or spears while running on logs! I was sure that they would have left me in a second had they gotten the chance.

Much to our delight, we discovered that we could talk to them, as they were speaking a dialect of the Citak language. The chief (who had become chief by killing the most people), whose name was Pau, sat down beside me. They were very suspicious of the bag I had and watched very carefully as I opened it and took out the gifts we had brought. We had things they had never seen before, such

Pau

as fishhooks, fish line, tin cans for water, a mirror, etc. I gave them to Pau to divide with the people. They made me empty everything I had in the bag for them to see, and one fellow "wrote" with my pen and another one tried on my hat.

Before leaving Senggo, I had coached Noak as to what we would say to the people if they understood the Citak language. The most thrilling experience of my missionary career was when Noak began to talk to them. He said, "The Person Who created you is named God. He lives up in the sky. He created the fish in the rivers, the wild boars, and the sago trees for you to eat. He created everything that you see. He also created us.

He is the One Who sent us here to tell you that He loves you."

Noak's speech seemed to frighten them. After all, they thought that we had just come straight from the Creator!

I had taken an Indonesian New Testament, and Noak explained to them that it was a "book" and that those figures in it were words. They all examined it, and then I gave it to Pau. I told him that the words in that Book were the Creator's Words and that we had come to explain to them the Words in that Book. I left the New Testament with them as a reminder that we would return.

All during this time, some of the men remained standing with their hands propped on the rafters beside their bow and arrows, which was a bit unnerving at times. At one point a man came running in from the jungle all excited and carrying his bow and arrows. A bit later he relaxed and put away his weapons.

Dominggus had been sitting, saying nothing since he did not understand the Citak language. After we had been there for some time, one man said to Noak, "We know that you are a man, and we know that he [Dominggus] is a man, but 'that thing'[me] is a white spirit, isn't it?"

Noak howled with laughter and told them that I was a human female. This disclosure was much to my dismay since I knew very well that on their raids against their enemy villages, they would kill the men and steal the women for themselves.

Then they brought food for us: sago, pork, sago grubs, and kangaroo rat. I had never before eaten rat, but when a crowd of affectionate headhunters said, "Eat it, eat it," I didn't feel like arguing. Besides, I had so many other things on my mind at that time that I hardly knew what I was eating at all.

After eating, we went outside to wait for the helicopter.

The people had calmed down a lot by then, so I gave them photos of Dominggus and me. I told them that they could look at them after we left and remember us. Then I showed them my camera and explained that I could get their "faces" with it so I could remember them. Several of them stood for me to "get their faces," but when I put the camera up to my eye, they ran like greased lightening back into the house. (Remember, their weapons were inside the house.)

At the same time, a man came up to me from behind and asked if the camera was something like a bow that I was going to shoot them with. I explained it all again. Then Noak stood with some of the very bravest warriors, and I took their picture. After that, others mustered up their courage and came out, and we took several pictures. By the time we left, they were posing.

We explained that the "flying canoe" (which they called the helicopter) was coming back and that we were going to

First trip

leave. We were not too sure whether or not we were indeed going to be allowed to leave, but at least we told them that we were. We assured them that we would return. Sedo, a big husky headhunter asked me if I would bring them some "skin" when I returned. It took a bit to understand that he was talking about clothes.

The helicopter returned and hovered above the logs. Dominggus and Noak ran ahead and climbed up into it, leaving me outside (and they didn't even know about "women's lib"!). Some of the Vakabuis men were helping me on the logs. When we got close to the helicopter, I showed the props to them and warned them about the danger. I told them to stop and let me go on alone. I was barefooted because, like the Citak people, I could wrap my toes around the logs and hang on a bit better. When I entered the wind from the props, it blew me off the log onto large sago thorns below. All this time, Jim was yelling for me to hurry, while Dominggus and Noak were seated comfortably inside the helicopter! I tried to get back on the log and was promptly blown off again. Finally, I ended up crawling on all fours on the log and climbed up into the helicopter in a very ungraceful manner with Dominggus pulling me inside!

The return to Senggo on the river boat was exciting. The motor wouldn't run, so we floated down river all day. The boat kept turning around and floating backward and kept going into the bushes along the sides of the river. So the men removed several floor boards which they used as paddles. The outhouse was made onto the back of the boat, and one time it was almost dragged off the boat—with Ruth in it!

When we arrived at the intersection and had begun to travel up river toward Senggo, we had to stop. They would not be able to paddle a 35-foot river boat against the current. We were very tired and spending another night on the boat wasn't anything to look forward to, but we had no choice. So we began to settle in for the night expecting that Clarence would come looking for us the next day.

About that time, a Muslim man happened by in a small canoe with a small motor. He took pity on Ruth and me and invited us to go with him. It was a miserable ride, squeezed in, and very slow, but a bit more appealing than the night on the boat. We arrived at Senggo about 2:00 a.m.—very tired and so happy to see our own beds.

When we arrived back at Senggo, the women were wailing and mourning for us like they do when someone dies. They were convinced that our reception at Vakabuis was not a welcome party, but that their chanting, dancing, and holding onto us showed their fear of us. A mistake on our part could have cost us our lives. They began begging us not to return to Vakabuis. They pantomimed cutting me up saying, "Those people are jungle people. They will kill you, cut off your arms and legs, cut off your head, and eat you." Very encouraging!

Noak said, "I am not going back." Titus also said the same thing.

I said, "I am not going back without one of them who can speak Citak faster than I."

More than two months later Noak came to me and said, "Nona, we must go back."

"That is just what I have been waiting to hear," I agreed.

We began making plans for our second trip to these precious people who were loved by God and for whom He died.

The Creator Has Come!

November 22, 1980

The second trip to Vakabuis included Clarence Gillett and pilot Jim Harris, along with Noak and me. We left to the sound of the women in Senggo mourning for us, as they were sure that we would never return. Since the Vakabuis people had thought I was a spirit, and thinking that Noak would be less fearful going without a "spirit," I offered to stay home.

Noak said, "No, Nona. They felt of you and know that you are human."

I thought, "Did they ever!"

Since no one takes women to war, it was decided that it would be safer if I went, and of course, I was delighted!

Jim gave Noak and me a lesson on "How to Close Helicopter Doors." It appeared that on that first trip we had hopped out leaving the back door open, creating a dangerous situation for Jim. In our excitement of jumping out of the helicopter, closing the door behind us had not been a priority.

As a safety precaution, the float plane flown by John Forsythe was to follow and circle overhead to be sure that we were all right. He would not have been able to land, but he could have buzzed overhead to frighten the people if necessary.

Float plane

As we neared the village, you can imagine our happy surprise when we looked down to see small poles placed on the ground as a helicopter landing pad. I knew then that we would receive a good reception.

Jim feared that the people might run into the props of the small helicopter, so the plan was for Clarence, Noak, and me to run right into the crowd, and since they would follow us, to draw them away from the helicopter. Clarence followed the plan! I was determined to see that the door was closed, but Noak was terrified and refused to turn loose of his escape route (the door). The people were trying to grab him to hug him, but he still wasn't too sure of them. He hung on to the door with all his might, and I finally had to leave him and go to the people. Eventually he calmed down, turned the door loose, and came to the people.

They immediately asked if we had brought bows to fight with, and we assured them that we did not come to fight and

Noak was afraid to turn loose of the helicopter.

had nothing with which to fight. They were afraid of the float plane that was circling overhead and kept yelling, "Make that thing go away. We don't want that thing." We motioned to Jim that all was well, and he turned off the motor of the helicopter. That was the signal to John that we were all right, and he then flew away.

When Jim stepped off the helicopter, they took one look at him and said, "There's the Creator!" After all, he had come from the sky, and that is where we had said God was. Later we learned that they thought that Clarence was God, so obviously they had not understood that God and the Creator were the same person.

On that first trip we did not see any women or children. This time some of the young boys appeared, and one brave little warrior about ten years old came out with his bow and arrows. Later when we were sitting in the house, he was sitting beside me, and I started to pat him on the leg. He fled in

Pilot Jim Harris

terror! So much for the "brave" young warrior!

I asked for the women, and they called out several old women. The young women and girls were still hiding. I asked the chief, Pau, where his wife was. He said she was hiding because she was afraid of "that thing." "That thing" was Jim.

Again, it was very difficult to get them to calm down enough to get very much across to them, but Noak did talk a bit. He told them that Jim and Clarence were human, but they wouldn't believe him.

I wanted to take pictures inside the house and showed them the flash and explained it to them. Then I pointed it toward myself and made it flash. They were terrified of it and kept yelling in no uncertain terms for me to put it back in my bag. The chief wouldn't touch it, but he took hold of my hand and made me put it back inside the bag. They kept yelling, "No fire. No fire." However, they didn't seem to mind our taking pictures outside.

We had certainly come to love these people and longed so much for the day when some of them would understand and enter the family of God. We

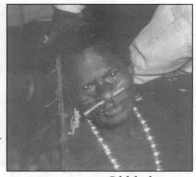

Old lady

were so grateful to God for the indescribable privilege of bringing the message of God's love to them for the very first time, and even as we left, we were already looking forward to the next visit.

Noak Preaches

March 4, 1981

After being postponed several times, Titus, Noak, Dominggus, and I made the third trip to Vakabuis on March 4, 1981. The pilot, John Miller, dropped us off about 8:30 a.m. and picked us up again about 2:30 p.m. We received a good reception, and as they had not seen Titus before, he got more than his share of hugs and Citak-style kisses—rubbing chins. I was happy to learn that that custom is reserved for men!

Rubbing chins

On this visit I was allowed to visit the houses. They were very unsteady "structures" built in the tree tops about 20 feet off the ground. I climbed up into one of them and visited with the women and children. However, several of the children ran away. Some of their ancestor's skulls were hanging in the house. They would put the corpses on a rack in front of the house; and when the flesh had decayed, they would save most of the bones—especially the skull. The skull was believed to ward off evil spirits.

Although the people had not gotten over their fear of the flash on the camera, they did allow me to take some pictures. I changed film with an old man pulling my hands away the entire time as he was afraid of what was inside the camera. I showed them pictures of themselves that I had taken on the last trip, and at first they just ignored them. Having no mirrors, they had never seen themselves, so of course, they didn't recognize themselves. When they recognized other people in the pictures, they became really excited.

Utan looking at pictures

I had brought coffee in a thermos. One fellow watched with great interest as I poured it into the cup while the others looked on, waiting for his verdict as to what it was. He looked up at the rest and announced, "It's diarrhea water!" I suddenly lost my appetite for coffee, and it took several weeks for me to regain it.

After much struggling, they figured out how to unscrew the top, and several of them stuck their fingers in it! We also had a picnic jug of red Kool-aid, and we decided it was best not to pour it out into the glasses where they could see it for fear that they would think we were drinking blood. We passed the jug around among ourselves and drank from it.

I had received mail on the float plane that morning and had it with me. As usual, they inspected everything I had and were impressed by it. I showed them a letter from my mother and explained that she lived a long way away, and I didn't get to see her. They wanted to know if she lived "down river," and I answered, "Yes." I showed them the words and told them that they were figures that she put down, and I could read them and know what she was doing. They examined it, got it very, very dirty, and even smelled it.

Besides the chief Pau, there were several others who seemed to stand out: Bidaw and Sedo (the two assistant chiefs), Wakin, Kanma, Utan, Esas, and others. In talking with them, we learned that Pau had killed and eaten six enemies and collected their skulls. Bidaw had two and was assistant chief because he had killed a man

Bidaw

who had tried to kill Pau. Pau enjoyed showing off the scars on his leg from the arrow wounds he had received. Sedo had three skulls, and he also really enjoyed showing the scars where an arrow had gone through his thigh. Sedo had three wives, two of whom had been stolen from enemy clans.

We had brought some clothes which they called "skin." Sedo had his arms in the legs of a pair of shorts trying to get them on over his head. Another man had his legs in a shirt, so we had a lesson on how to put on clothes. Noak had given a young fellow a pair of shorts on our last trip, but he was still naked. We asked him where his shorts were, and he said, "In the house." I guess he was saving them for Sunday!

They had a lovely sense of humor and loved to tease. We would take small packets of salt as gifts, and they loved it from the very first. On this trip we were all sitting on the floor, and I was giving out the packets. I gave one to groups of three to four. When I finished, the first group indicated that I had not given them any. I was sure I had, but they were spreading out their empty hands, and knowing they had no pockets, I wondered where they had put the packets. Then I picked up a leg, and there it was! They hooted with laughter and seemed to love it that I figured it out.

They were going to kill a pig for a feast for us, and I wanted to take pictures of the chase. The man ran across the logs just as if it were level ground, shot the pig with bow and arrow on the run, and killed it with the first shot. I was still focusing the camera and missed the entire thing. That was when I realized that if they decided to kill us, running would be foolish!

The best part of the trip was Noak's talk to them. We had Bible pictures, and I had planned to hold the pictures while Noak talked. I am sure that about everything we did was strange to them, and it was no wonder that they were still a bit frightened at times. Noak asked them to sit quietly while he stood in front of them to speak. When I stood up to hold the pictures, several of them ran away, and others yelled at the children to run away as they thought we were about to perform some kind of witchcraft. Since they didn't seem to be as afraid of Titus, I sat back down with the people, and he held the pictures as Noak told the story.

They were excited when they recognized the crocodile in the pictures of creation. Then they recognized the fish, the birds, and the snake. To them the lion was a pig, and the giraffe was a kangaroo rat!

It is impossible to describe, but everyone was talking at once, and many weren't listening at all. Still, some were very, very interested! It was bedlam. Utan, especially, stood up with Noak and Titus and kept interrupting and repeating everything Noak said.

After talking about how God had created all the things they saw and ate and about how sin entered the world, Noak talked about "God's village." He told them that people didn't fight, nor kill, nor get sick or hungry, and that nobody died. Naturally, they thought that was a pretty nice place, and what seemed to impress them the most was that people don't fight there. They were greatly impressed with the miracles of Christ, especially about His healing the blind man and raising the dead.

Utan continued to repeat everything that he said. After hearing about the blind man being healed, he would close his eyes and say, "He was blind like this?" And then he would open his eyes and say, "And then he could see like this?"

They wanted to know if Noak could raise people from the dead. What impressed them the most was that Jesus could walk on the water and not sink!

I wish I could describe the expressions on their faces when Noak told about the death of Jesus. They kept saying over and over, "He didn't do anything wrong. He didn't make any mistakes at all."

When we told them that Jesus never did anything wrong, they asked, "They killed Him anyway?" Then they wanted to know if it was "earth people" (humans) who had killed Him.

Noak and me with the Vakabuis people

The resurrection didn't sound so strange to them. After all, they believed that the spirits of their ancestors were all around them. We explained to them that Jesus' body rose from the dead. Then they would hold our arms and ask, "This stuff came back to life, too?" They asked if He rose by magic, and Noak told them no, that He rose because He was God's Son and that He could do anything He wanted to do.

While Noak was talking, they had the pig heart and liver on the fire along with some sago. They took it off and put it on the floor. Dozens of small roaches were crawling all over it! I kept my eye on a piece of liver that was on top of the pile and was pretty sure that not too many roaches had gotten up that far. I don't like liver, but I was determined to get that piece.

Before eating, Noak told them to close their eyes, and we would talk to God and thank Him for the food. Most of them weren't too thrilled about that as they thought it was some kind of magic, but two or three of them practiced closing their eyes, saying, "Amen," then opening them again. Since they were afraid, we told them just to keep their eyes open and not talk, and we would close our eyes and talk to God. They couldn't keep quiet, though, and discussed with much excitement what we were doing all through the prayer. They were excited when Noak prayed for them. After the prayer they kept asking, "Does He hear you?"

As soon as the prayer was over, I grabbed the bamboo knife and cut off my piece of liver. But Pau, the chief, immediately grabbed it from me. At first I was afraid that I had done something offensive, but he pinched off a piece of it with his filthy dirty hands, handed it to a young man with equally dirty hands who ate it, and then gave the meat back to me. I learned later that this was to prove to me that no curse had been put on the food. If they had only known that it wasn't witchcraft that I was afraid of!

John was late coming back to pick us up. It was very hot and humid, and we were all getting tired and sleepy when a man said to me, "Just close your eyes and tell him to come back." He still thought that the pilot was God.

We continued to pray that the day would soon come when they would not only understand Who God was and His love for them, but they would also come to trust Him for salvation.

CHAPTER

Rumors of War

July 13, 1981

This was a special trip as we took along summer workers, Keith and Terri Rascher. Keith was a missionary kid (MK) who had grown up in Irian Jaya. He and Terri later returned to Irian Jaya as career missionaries. We went by boat nine hours up the Brazza River to where I thought we were to meet the helicopter. You can imagine our disappointment when we arrived to discover that the village huts, Zurasamur, had fallen to the ground and that the people had moved. We were rained on most of the day, so we were very wet and tired. Then Noak, who knew all along that the village had moved, felt it would be good to tell us that we would have to continue on up the river to find the people!

We went on up and arrived about 5:30 p.m., just as it was getting dark. We were greeted by a group of men on the river banks with their bows and arrows. One man shot a warning shot across the river in front of us. I recognized only one man, but when they saw Noak, they recognized him, so we were received. We quickly hung the radio antenna as we were due to call Senggo at 5:30 p.m. Clarence asked if there was any fighting going on there, and we asked the men who had met us.

They all said, "No, nobody is fighting here."

Since Clarence had heard rumors of a war in the area, he

told us to ask again if anyone else in the area was fighting.

They again answered, "Nobody in the area is fighting."

We reported to Clarence, turned off the radio for the night, climbed up about 20 feet into the tree house and immediately saw two men with recent arrow wounds! Then they admitted that they had been attacked by a village upriver a couple of weeks before. The whole thing was a linguistic error. I had asked them if anyone **is** fighting, and since they were not fighting at that **exact** time, they answered, "No."

At first they refused to say why they had been attacked, but later someone told me a very interesting story about how the people from the upriver village had stolen two of their women. The Zurasamur men killed one of the upriver village men during the attack on them and admitted to eating him. However, they did want me to understand and kept saying, "We didn't kill him; we just finished him off. His own people killed him."

It took a while to get the story straight, but a man from the enemy village had climbed up the poles expecting the people inside the house to be sleeping. They woke up and began shooting their arrows at him. He began to scramble back down the poles. In the process, his friends thought he was one of the Zurasamur men and shot him and ran away. However, they did not kill him, so the Zurasamur people finished him off and ate him. It seems that whoever disables the person gets "credit" for killing him, and his own people had done that!

Of course, it was dark by then and too late to report to Clarence, and we had nowhere else to go so we decided unanimously to stay! Staying in the house with "friendly" headhunters expecting to be attacked at any moment sounded better that staying alone in the middle of the jungle.

Our accommodations certainly couldn't be called a home away from home! The house measured about 20 by 30 feet, one room, and was between 20 and 25 feet in the treetops. I counted 43 people in it that first night and not even one bath! There were eight fireplaces which meant that eight families lived there. The fireplaces were just piles of dirt on the floor with the fires on them.

Terri was being broken into missionary life in the jungle in a big hurry. We were not about to attempt to climb down the poles in the middle of the night to use the "facilities," so "when in Zurasamur, do as the Zurasamur people do." Climbing the poles was a challenge in the daytime, but it was terrifying in the middle of the night! We feared that the Zurasamur people themselves might mistake us for the enemy and shoot us.

The people were obviously nervous. There was another house there, and Noak went over to visit in the other one. When he returned and was climbing the poles, they made him identify himself. Whenever they heard any noise, they would all run to the doorway or to cracks in the walls. The walls were palm fronds, and they had bows and arrows hidden in a place in the wall.

We ate and then began to prepare for the night. The house was hot and very

Tree house where we stayed

smoky, so I decided to put my sleeping bag in the doorway where, hopefully, I could breathe some fresh air. One fellow was very helpful and helped Terri with her sheet and practically tucked her in. I was already on my sleeping bag when he told me to move to another place. It was very near a fire, and I said that I didn't want to sleep there. He reached over and took me by the waist, almost picked me up, and said, "If those enemies come, they will come in that doorway, pick you up like this, and take you away!" His was not too pleasant a bed-time story! But I was sure that I would die if I tried to sleep near the fires in the middle of the room with all the smoke, humidity, and odors. I felt that I would rather take my chances on being carried away than to sleep so close to the fire, so I stayed where I was.

Nobody slept that night, and I mean nobody! People talked, babies cried, women kept putting wood on the fires, and Keith either had a dog sleeping on his sleeping bag with him, or else his neighbor at his head decided to use his pillow with him, or his neighbor at his feet didn't give room for his feet. The one at his feet was thoughtful, though, and wanted Keith to stretch out and prop his feet on the fellow's chest!

The next morning we packed up, carried our things down out of the house, put them in the boat, and prepared for Jim to come in the helicopter to take us in to Vakabuis. Jim called to tell us the sad news that the helicopter battery was dead and would not take a charge. He would have to wait for one to be brought in from Sentani on the north coast. It was late morning before we finally knew that he would not be in that day and that we would have to spend another "lovely" night with the friendly headhunters in the "Brazza Hilton."

We spent the day sitting around on logs and visiting with the people. Once that afternoon Noak was followed to the jungle where he had gone to relieve himself and was accused of going to flirt with their women. Noak had to prove that he had been to relieve himself by showing them the evidence!

One fellow thought it was his responsibility to keep Terri

happy so he spent a lot of time with his arm around her! Keith asked me to remind him that she was his wife!

Most of the people had several small holes in their nose, and we learned that what I had thought to be straws or sticks in them as decorations were actually bones from bat wings. I got a small thorn in my finger, so a man removed a bone from his nose, picked out my thorn, and put the bone back in its place!

That night was mostly a repeat of the night before. We popped popcorn which we had brought with us, and they loved it. They kept asking for more, so we had to make three pots full—the sum total of all that we had brought.

That night the water level went down in the river, and Noak went out to put the boat down off the bank into the water where it was leaning precariously. When he returned, one of the men yelled at him and accused him of stealing something and taking it out. Noak calmly explained what he had been doing, and they seemed to accept it. We learned quickly that we should always explain ahead of time what we were doing.

The next morning Jim came for us and took us in for a short visit to Vakabuis. When we arrived, they asked me if Noak was going to tell them God's Word again, and when I said, "Yes," they began to dance and chant. They really liked Noak and called him "Ndoak."

They kept asking, "What was the name of the Creator?" and "What was the name of the Man Who healed the blind man?" They promised to put those names into their foreheads and not forget them again.

Terri and I went over to the house where the women were gathered. When they saw us coming, they ran out and hugged us and began introducing themselves. That was very different from anything we had seen of the women thus far.

We were winning their confidence and believed that God was going to build His church in this village. We longed for the day when some of these people would join the family of God. We needed to find a way to have a more regular witness to them.

CHAPTER

Pau's Helicopter Ride

July 1981–December 1982

During this period of time, we were encouraging the people to stop fighting and to move to the edge of a river large enough so we could get in by motor boat. The cost of using the helicopter prevented us from making more frequent trips. We were also praying for a Citak evangelist who would be willing to move to Vakabuis, live there, and teach the people on a regular basis.

It was during this time also, that the first people from Vakabuis came to Senggo. That visit was exciting. They all flocked into my house, and you can't imagine their interest in everything! I had a glass candy dish in the shape of a chicken. They were afraid of it and screamed when I took off the lid (the top of the chicken)!

I went in to the bedroom to round up ones who had wandered all over the house and found one man admiring himself from all sides in front of the large mirror. Then I returned to the living room to a naked man sitting cross-legged in the middle of the dining table! Their visit was fun.

We continued making periodic trips to the villages of Vakabuis, Esaun, and Serai in that area. Some men from Serai also visited Senggo. During that trip I gave a nice knife to the chief, Boar.

Our General Director, Dr. Richard Winchell, visited

Senggo in September 1981 and it was our joy to take him up
to visit our friends at Vakabuis. I enjoyed introducing "my
chief" to "their chiefs."

*My "chief," Dr. Richard Winchell,
meets their chiefs, Pau and Bidaw*

Clarence made a trip to Vakabuis during this period, and
the following account was taken from his report:

■ ■ ■

"We spent the night in the village of Binam, while the
men with me spent the night in the village houses. In their
conversation they got news of things that were going on up
the Brazza River, and they woke up the next morning saying
they didn't want to go on.

"Titus Fiak in particular was really scared. They had heard
a number of stories from the Brazza River about fighting that
had been going on recently. The report was that two villages,
Lower Vautu and Pirabanak, were fighting each other. Lower

Vautu was getting ready to come down and fight Pirabanak. The village of Vautu had been raided, and a number of people had been killed. Baskap also had been raided, and a number of them had been killed by the non-Citak village, Butu.

"I said, 'Look, we have this big boat, (the 35-foot river boat) which has a steel hull. If things look hostile, we will just turn around and come back, but we're going to go up and take a look and see how it is.' We went on up and when we arrived at Pirabanak, we discovered that they were not fighting and were at peace with Vautu, so there was nothing to worry about there.

"So we went on up to Vautu, who was supposed to be preparing for an attack on Pirabanak, but they obviously weren't preparing any attack and were very friendly! When we arrived at Lower Vautu, we were immediately invited in and fed sago and treated really well. When we asked them about the attack, they answered that another section of the village located further up river had been attacked and several people had been killed, but they were not sure of the number.

"When we arrived at the upper Vautu, we learned that nine people had been killed, two adult women and seven children. They said that the people who had killed them had caught them in the bivouacs. They had dismembered them leaving the torsos and taking the heads, arms, and legs of all nine with them. They accused the Vakabuis people of doing it. That was quite interesting and concerned me because we planned to go to Vakabuis by helicopter the next day.

"By then it was dark, so we put a Petromax gas lamp on top of the boat, so we could see any logs that may be floating on the river, and kept going on up river until about nine o'clock. I thought we had passed Baskap and figured that we would be safe so we tied up to the side of the river for the night.

"The next morning we arrived at our final destination, the village of Zurasamur. Several villages, Sepana, Batizawin, Sinamur, and Baskap, had gathered there to form an alliance to repel the enemies in their area. We were well received there.

"When the helicopter arrived, three other fellows—Titus Fiak, Sahu Fiak, and Frans Isaka—got in to go to Vakabuis. We planned that if there was any hostility at all, we would not even get out of the helicopter. We also agreed that we would not even mention the village of Vautu.

"We were received well. The people had their hair tied up in little ribbons of native string and were in a festive mood. We could tell that there had been some kind of festivity going on. Sahu and Titus were given the chin-rubbing welcome. When the question of war came up, someone ran over to the wall of the long house we were in, quickly grabbed an old shield, broke it, and said, 'We don't have any more war. We don't fight any more here.'

"When we were getting ready to leave, the pilot, John Miller, wanted to experiment setting the helicopter down on a couple of logs. I said, 'While you're doing that, why don't you take Pau and maybe Bidaw for a ride? I think they would enjoy that.' I explained it to Pau and Bidaw, but didn't think to explain it to the others. Then Sedo also wanted to ride, so I put Pau in the front and was about to put Sedo and Bidaw in the back when suddenly two men came running out from the house and opened the door and tried to pull Pau out. We tried to explain to them that the helicopter was just going to move over to a different spot. I finally had to just push the people away and tell John to get going. He did, and Pau had a short ride.

"However, Titus was having his own bit of excitement in the house. When Pau got in the helicopter and we closed the door, the people in the house grabbed their bows and arrows from the rafters, and others grabbed Titus. One had him by the neck, and others grabbed him by the arms. Of course, it only lasted for a short time as they soon realized that Pau was not being taken away, but Titus was pretty shaken.

"From Vakabuis, we flew to Esaun. That was the first real contact these people had had with the outside. We had a good visit with them.

"When we arrived back to where we had left the river boat, it was gone! We flew down river and found it and learned that the men we had left on it had had their own bit of excitement while we were at Vakabuis and Esaun. The Zurasamur people were all over the boat, and Frans, perhaps not too kindly, told them to move. The people were very unhappy, quickly got off the boat, ran into the jungle and picked up bows and arrows and lined up along the river bank. So our men unplugged the radio, leaving the antenna and paddled off down river to safety."

■ ■ ■

Now back to our story. Different ones continued to make periodic visits to Vakabuis, Esaun, and Serai; and they did finally move down to the edge of the Beau River. Up until that point, none of us had ever spent the night in the village. Ruth Dougherty and I felt it was time for us to spend some time with them.

CHAPTER

A Brief Stay at Vakabuis

December 31, 1982 – January 13, 1983

We had waited a long time for this experience, and finally on December 31, 1982, Ruth Dougherty, Piet Bakasu (a Senggo paramedic), Titus Fiak, Yakub Fiak (Noak's younger brother), and I returned to Vakabuis and spent 12 nights with the Vakabuis people, which was a never-to-be-forgotten experience.

We flew by float plane to the village of Binam, located at the mouth of the Beau River where Vakabuis is located. We spent the night there, and the next day we hired six Binam men with two canoes to paddle us up river to Vakabuis. The trip took six and one-half hours.

Earlier, Clarence had sent Frans Isaka and Habel Kermek, two Senggo men, to Vakabuis to build a house for Frans and his wife. Then they were to move there and serve as their evangelist. Frans and Habel stayed only two nights and returned to Senggo reporting to us that the Vakabuis people were going to kill them. We were not too concerned about this as the Senggo people often do this when they first go out to live in another village, and it usually turns out that they are just homesick. So we had planned to take Frans back with us, but when it came time to leave Senggo, he had run away to the jungle, obviously so he would not have to go.

When we neared Vakabuis, we could hear their excited voices around the curve in the river. As we came into sight and they recognized who we were, they did their usual shouting, chanting, and dancing routine and gave us a good welcome.

The first three nights were miserable—to say the least. I am sure I have never spent more miserable nights. Ruth and I slept in our tents which were indescribably hot. The first night six men proceeded to build three fires in front of the tent and set up guard there. They coughed, slapped mosquitoes, and talked all night. So we decided that we might as well not sleep either! We weren't sure if they were guarding us from enemy attack or guarding us in case we might try to do something.

We got our answer the next night when they asked permission not to sleep, or stay, near us because it was too cold, and the mosquitoes were too bad. We gladly gave them permission not to guard us!

Then that night Ruth and I caused a commotion ourselves. We had put a very large piece of plastic on poles in order to collect rain water. In the middle of the night it began to rain, and we both jumped off our sleeping bags and ran out of the tent to put the bucket under it. I dived back into the tent first and about tore it down when I discovered that it was inhabited. I was scared half to death. It was just a poor, cold doggy who had found a nice warm place to sleep—on Ruth's sleeping bag! He didn't want to leave, but with considerable persuasion, we got him out. The next day we discovered that the men were all ready to come and rescue us from the enemy clans until they heard us laughing. It was comforting to know that they were prepared to protect us.

We asked the people to complete Frans' house for us, and

Our tents and water-collection plastic

they went right to work. Deceit is a way of life for them, and they seemed to expect it of us. Someone would come several times a day to ask me again what we were going to give them for building the house. I named all the things that I would give them and repeated over and over again that we would keep our word and would not lie to them.

This continued for the three days it took them to build the house. I was a bit apprehensive about this, not knowing what their reaction would be when I gave them the promised items.

A house built in three days should more realistically be called a "shelter." It was made from poles tied together with vines, with palm fronds for the roof and walls. The walls were about three and one-half feet high.

After the house was finished, we had a big to-do and I

asked them to repeat to me what I had promised to give them—machete, fish line, fish hooks, shorts, etc. As they named the items, I would lay them down in front of Pau, the chief, for him to divide. They were very pleased, and no doubt a bit surprised that we actually did what we had promised.

It had rained very hard the last night we spent in the

Our "mansion"

tents, and we slept on a literal "water bed." It was a very long night. We moved into the house at 5:00 a.m.! The people couldn't understand why we didn't want them to sleep with us. Apparently it is part of their hospitality code to sleep with guests. We made a "partition" about three feet high from palm fronds down the middle of the house and with considerable encouragement (some in the form of taking them by the hand and leading them), we got them to stay on the other side with Piet, Titus, and Yakub. That is, all except Pau, who refused to budge. He rarely left our side the entire time except for the night, even sleeping during the day at Ruth's feet.

The first few days were quite miserable as the people gave us absolutely no privacy. We got lots of practice changing clothes under the sheets. It was very hot, and the flies were unbearable. We put up a mosquito net to eat under, which helped.

Every afternoon we entertained the people by another strange custom of ours, taking a bath. This was done fully clothed in the river with the villagers on the bank no doubt wondering what in the world that strange ritual meant. The first day Pau proceeded to get in the river with us—upriver from us, much to our dismay! He began to imitate us. He had never seen soap, so we soaped ourselves. I then handed him the soap. He soaped up his face, got it in his eyes, and that was the end of the "bathing-with-a-friend" episode. From then on, he was content to stand on the safety of the bank with everyone else and just watch.

One day we went on an all-day trip into the jungle to get sago with Bidaw and his family. From that day on, their nightly entertainment was mimicking Ruth and me pounding the sago fibers with the special stick made for that purpose.

During the 12 days we were there, we had a variety of interesting food: tree

Bidaw and family

kangaroo, wild pork, jungle rat, lizard, fish, turtle, grub worms, sago, heart of palm, etc. I wonder what some of that would taste like with the Colonel's recipe! Ruth and I almost parted friendship on Sunday. I had planned the menu for that day and had been looking forward to it ever since we had arrived. I had planned to have rice and canned corned beef brought with us from Senggo, and my mouth was watering with anticipation. However, someone showed up that morning with a "nice" gift of jungle rat, and Ruth, not wanting to waste such a gift, insisted that we eat it instead of the corned beef. I insisted that we go with the plan to eat corned beef. Ruth insisted that the corned beef would save, but that the rat would spoil. That was exactly what I wanted it to do!

Ruth holds one of her appetizing friends, a kangaroo rat!

Ruth won the argument, showing little respect to the fact that I was the senior missionary. We ate rat! After all, you can eat canned corned beef any day, but you can't get nice jungle rat every day!

One interesting thing that happened was that an Indonesian trader had been there and had told the people that the "man above the trees" wanted them to smoke. Obviously, he meant for them to believe that the man was God. He used tobacco to trade with. However, he was not aware that they believe that a world of spirits live just above the tree tops. They thought the man was one of their spirits. We could see God's hand in this as it would have been difficult if we were teaching them not to smoke and if someone else were telling them that God wanted them to. Pau was a heavy smoker of native leaves. When I told him that smoking would make him sick and would make him die early, he accused me of lying.

About two days later he came down with an attack of asthma, pneumonia, and pleurisy. He was very, very sick and coughed almost constantly. Ruth, who is a nurse, examined him; and after Piet gave him penicillin shots, he got better. He seemed to be very impressed by that, and as far as we know, he did not smoke anymore while we were there.

There was a four-year-old boy in the village who had been stolen from another clan after they had killed and eaten his mother. They were now rearing him as their own. Several women, stolen in wars with other clans, were there as wives of the men who had stolen them. The people seemed so mild and had such a lovely sense of humor that it was hard for us to believe that they could be such warriors. They assured us over and over that they intended to build a regular village there and not run into the jungle again and that they didn't intend to fight anymore.

The people were very open and receptive to anything we had to say. All of us experienced real frustration in presenting the Gospel to them. Imagine that you are one of those people seeing someone from the outside for the first time, and these strange people come and tell you that Someone Who lives up in the sky somewhere and is called God created you. He has a nice village up there where people live forever and are never sick, nor hungry, nor sad. He loves you and wants you to go there and live with Him forever, but He will not allow even the least sin to enter His nice village. Since you have sinned, you are excluded. However, He opened a "path" for you to come. He sent His Son Whose name is Jesus. He became a human and never did anything wrong. Wicked men killed Him, and He rose again from the dead. Now if you believe that and believe that His Son died just to take your punishment for your sin, and if you confess to Him that you are a sinner, He will remove all your sins and will let you live with Him forever in His Village.

They would ask me,

- "Was Jesus from your tribe?"
- "Did He speak your language?"
- "Did you ever see Him?"

When I answered, "No," to all those questions, their looks would say, "This is foolish!" It seemed impossible that they could understand that, and it would have been impossible except for the Holy Spirit.

We would tell them stories about Jesus, and they enjoyed hearing about the miracles, but when we came to the substitutionary death of Christ, it seemed as if we had a barrier in front of us keeping us from believing that they could ever understand. However, we knew that, as difficult as it may seem, we must tell it. We believed that the Holy Spirit would open their hearts, and we prayed that He would do just that.

We used the Indonesian word "Surga" for Heaven, and they thought it was Senggo, and that we had come straight from God. Others still thought that the airplane and helicopter came down from Heaven.

One day when I was telling them about the resurrection of Christ and was emphasizing that it was a bodily resurrection, I told them that Jesus ate fish and sago. Bidaw added, "And wild boar and grub worms."

The village of Esaun had also moved down on the same

river, and we had hoped to visit there, but it was too far away for us to paddle. However, most of the men from that village came down to Vakabuis to meet us.

We were even more concerned that God would call some-one from Senggo who would be willing to make the sacrifices necessary to go and live with these people and to minister to them. So far, they wanted to go IF we went, but they wanted to return to Senggo when we did. Some were afraid to live there, and others were just not ready to accept the inconven-iences of living there.

7

CHAPTER

Diary Entries

February 17, 1983 to February 23, 1983

THURSDAY: Gail Vinje (TEAM nurse at Senggo), Sahu Fiak (Titus' older brother), Yakub Fiak (Noak's younger brother), and I were picked up by John Forsythe with the float plane and taken to Binam. We had a bit of trouble getting the Binam people to loan us a canoe and to paddle us to Vakabuis, but we finally got off about 11:15 a.m. Since our last trip had taken six and one-half hours, we expected to arrive at Vakabuis about 6:00 p.m. or before. Darkness falls right about 6:00 p.m., and we didn't want to arrive after dark.

However, the water was higher and the current much stronger, so we didn't arrive until about 7:15 p.m. As we neared the village, we shined our flashlights on ourselves and began calling to them so they would know it was us and not be frightened into shooting us. We were given our usual warm and noisy welcome, and everything seemed just great.

■ ■ ■

FRIDAY was a normal Vakabuis day. We had them build a shelter for our cooking fire, and we also had them repair the roof on the house. We put up our plastic for catching rain water. The people were more demanding than usual, wanting knives and shorts for small pieces of sago which we usually bought with a couple of fishhooks. They also were more

Pau and family going out for food

brazen in their attempts at stealing.

Bidaw had a jungle fruit that tasted a bit like a green apple. He had only one which he peeled with his hatchet. He looked at Gail, then at me, then at the fruit. It was obvious that he wanted to give it to us but had only one. So he put it in his mouth and bit it in two. He then gave the one half to Gail and took the other half out of his mouth and handed it to me! I wondered why he didn't use the hatchet. We ate it.

■ ■ ■

SATURDAY: Gail and I went into the jungle with Bidaw and his family and spent the day getting sago, leaving Sahu and Yakub in the village with our belongings. We went down-river a ways by canoe and then walked about 20 minutes into the swampy jungle to the sago trees. I got 20 leeches in 20 minutes on the way in and 13 on the way out. Gail spent so much time slipping in the mud that the leeches had a harder time getting through the mud to her, so she didn't get as many.

Gail and some of her new friends

Being short, she kept getting left behind and had to yell for the rest of us to wait for her. Bidaw enjoyed teasing her and would yell back at her, "You were the one who said, 'I want to go,' so come on and catch up."

They didn't finish processing the sago until very late, and then a storm began to come up. We went as quickly as possible back out of the jungle, but a very hard rain hit us just as we got to the canoes. We were going against a very swift current and a hard rain and didn't get back to the village until after 7:00 p.m.—over an hour after dark.

Sahu and Yakub were frightened out of their wits, thinking that we had been killed in the jungle. We had the single-side band radio with us in order to keep in contact with Senggo, and they had tried to use it to call Senggo but didn't know how to work it. Sahu had been crying, and Yakub was very, very angry with us. He told us in no uncertain terms that we didn't come to hunt sago and that we were not to leave the village again. His anger was from fear. It says a lot for them that they stayed in the village and didn't run away; although, they were, no doubt, very frightened. We felt really bad that we had caused them so much worry. We apologized and promised to teach them to use the radio and not to leave again.

The people continued to try to steal almost constantly. I told them that they were not to come on our side of the house again. I could have saved my breath! They were not about to listen to the likes of me! So I told them that if they continued to steal, that we would not buy anything else from them or give them anything else. We would normally buy such things as firewood, fish, sago, or whatever else we could. That was when trouble actually began, although it wasn't openly shown right then.

Their thoughts no doubt had already been brewing even before that because as early as Friday, one of the men told me that we had to leave all our belongings there when we left, including our own personal clothing, etc. We had a fish net with us which we tied up down the river to catch fish for eating. We normally caught enough to share with the people, and they were fascinated with the lovely net. On Saturday Bidaw told me that we had to leave our fish net there, which we had already planned to do.

Also, some people from Esaun had arrived with their chief, Boar, on Saturday and came looking for us as we were coming from the jungle. Bidaw whispered to me that they were angry because they had not gotten things from us and that I was not to give them anything. We passed this off without much thought because we were used to them not wanting to share their things with anyone else.

■ ■ ■

SUNDAY: That morning I again made some of them leave our side of the house. I reported to Senggo on the radio early in the morning that all was fine. Within a few minutes of that, Yakub told me that the people didn't want to come for a service. I realized that trouble was brewing and immediately turned on the radio. Expecting no one to have his radio on since it was Sunday, I was thrilled to hear the pilots having a meeting. I asked them to stand by and asked Gail to stay by the radio.

Things then moved so quickly that a seemingly normal situation turned into a very dangerous one. A group of men led by Pau came into the house. Pau said that we had to lay out all our things, the trade goods as well as our own personal belongings which included the clothes we were wearing, and to divide them among the villagers.

I said, "No," so they said that they would not listen to God's Word. They were becoming more and more agitated, but I said that we would not pay them to listen to God's Word, and since we had come for that purpose, if they did not want that, then we would leave.

The people immediately went into an attitude of war—dancing, chanting, and beating on the walls. I put my hands on Pau's shoulders and asked him to calm down and listen to what I had to say. At first he tried to shove me away, and he actually swung at me, but his hand went over my head. I feared that we were about to be killed.

I kept talking and finally he quieted down. When he quieted down, everyone else did also. Then they all sat down.

I went over again, as we had done many times before, why we had come into their village to begin with and why we were there now. I reminded them that we had come, never with weapons and never to fight, but only because we loved them and wanted them to know that God loved them.

They would say among themselves, "That's right; she loves us; that's right; they never brought weapons and never came to fight."

I explained to them the importance of their souls over the things that we could give them. They seemed to be very receptive. Then Sahu preached on the death of Christ. While Sahu was preaching, I went across to the radio and called Ken Dresser at Senggo to explain what had happened. I then saw that the people were becoming very restless, so I motioned to Sahu to cut his message short. He finished quickly, and most of the men jumped up immediately and ran off to their canoes and began paddling madly downstream.

Pau

The main agitators in the uprising were Pau, Bidaw, and Boar, the chief from Esaun. On our previous trip there, the Esaun people had been offended because they didn't get as many things from us as they had wanted. They had told some of the Vakabuis people that they didn't want to hear God's Word because of that reason. Making threats like that is normal, so we didn't think much about it at the time, especially as more Esaun people came to Vakabuis after that to visit with us. There didn't seem to be any problem.

We were surprised and very disappointed to see Bidaw practically leading the agitation. He had always been very friendly and receptive and seemed to understand more than some of the others of our purpose in being there. There was a group who were not involved at all in the fracas, including

Sedo and an older widower named Dasawu. They didn't stand up for us but quietly got out of the way showing that they were not involved.

When the group left for the jungle, we learned that they were going for war arrows. They didn't need many to kill just the four of us and certainly didn't need to go for more, so at first we didn't understand this.

We had been keeping constant contact with both John Forsythe, the float plane pilot, and with the helicopter pilots, as well with Ken Dresser, the Senggo station head. They were preparing for a possible emergency evacuation. John Forsythe could have gotten to us the quickest, but he could not land as the river was too small. However, he could fly low to scare the people if necessary until the helicopter could get there.

We talked about it among ourselves and with some of the people in the village. We decided to wait until the people returned from getting their arrows to see what their attitude would be. We expected they would return no later than 3:00 p.m.—still leaving time for the helicopter to get to us if necessary. We realized that we were taking a chance on their killing us immediately upon their return, but the ones not involved in the trouble and who were still in the village felt that we would be safe, so we felt we were making the right decision to stay.

We could not have left by canoe, as we would have had to go past where they were and felt that they would not have allowed us to go.

This no doubt was pretty tough on Gail. It was her first trip to Vakabuis, and not understanding the Citak language, much of the time she didn't know what was happening.

When we heard the canoes coming, Sahu, Yakub, and I went out to the river bank to meet them while Gail stayed by the radio. They arrived with the makings for what seemed like enough arrows to kill off several clans. However, they all seemed friendly except for Pau. I talked first with Bidaw, who said that they felt sad about what had happened and that it was all over and that they were not going to fight us.

Sahu and I then went to Pau, and as we talked, he also warmed up. He said that I was their "mother" as I had been the first to come into their village. He shared some heart of palm with us and told me that he would give me the arrows he was making. He told us not to pay any attention to what people were saying. We had not heard the people say anything, but we were curious to know what it was.

An older widower, Dasawu, invited Sahu and Yakub to go pig hunting with some of them on Tuesday. All seemed well, and we reported this invitation to the folks at Senggo and to the pilots. We felt that their friendliness was genuine.

MONDAY: Everyone seemed to be going out of his way to be nice to us. They stayed out of our side of the house, mostly, and we didn't feel that we had to watch our stuff as closely as before. They kept asking us if we were going to stay. We told them that we were staying until Thursday as planned. They told us that they would be afraid to do anything to us as they couldn't run and hide in the treetops again as our helicopter could find them. They said that they had gotten so many arrows because they thought we were calling in forces to protect us, and they were preparing to defend themselves.

All seemed well, and we were planning to keep to our original plan to leave on Thursday morning by canoe with several of the Vakabuis people to help paddle us back to Binam. We planned to spend the night at Binam where the float plane would pick us up and take us back to Senggo on Friday.

TUESDAY: They had recently built their long house which housed the unmarried men and widowers just a few feet from our house. The men in it would stay awake all night slapping mosquitoes, keeping the fires going, and talking, usually very loud. We were used to it, so usually we tried to tune it out in order to get some sleep ourselves. Yakub came to me early in the morning and told me that he woke up in the early hours and heard Dasawu, the older widower, discussing us. He was saying that Sahu and Yakub would have to be killed, and that Gail and I would be taken, obviously as their wives.

Dasawu

That news was a bit unnerving to say the least, and it didn't sound any too pleasant for any of us. We reported it to Ken at Senggo at 7:30 a.m. By then most of the people had gone out into the jungle for the day. Dasawu and his friends had already gone to hunt pigs. Needless to say, Sahu and Yakub had turned down the invitation to go with them!

Ken at Senggo, John Forsythe (the float pilot at Yawsakor), and Jim Harris (the helicopter pilot at Wamena) were all standing by for an emergency evacuation. Several options were being explored. The MAF helicopter could only bring two of us out at a time which could possibly result in some danger for the two who were left for the second shuttle. No other helicopter was available. They discussed bringing in police to stay with the ones who would wait for the second shuttle.

We at Vakabuis felt that a dramatic evacuation would hinder our returning to the village as the people there would either be hostile or would run back into the jungle where we could not find them again. We did not want any police for fear that they would kill some of the Vakabuis people and destroy all the trust we had built.

We considered leaving immediately by canoe and telling the people that we had to return to Senggo. However, some of the Vakabuis people themselves would have to paddle us to Binam. We did not feel that we could get a clear assessment of the situation from Sahu and Yakub. Yakub was clearly very frightened. Sahu kept saying, "I'm not afraid. If I die, it doesn't matter, but I'm just thinking about you and Gail." We were sure that he was more frightened than he wanted to admit.

Up until then, Ken, our station head at Senggo, had been leaving all decisions up to me. Then we came up with the "perfect" solution. We reported this idea to Ken at Senggo. We said that we would go ahead and spend the night there. Early the next morning, we would load our stuff in the canoe. Then we would report in on the radio just as we were ready to leave. Gail and I would get in the canoe with paddlers from Vakabuis to paddle us to Binam, and then Yakub and Sahu would climb the trees and take down the antenna at the very last. When we were sure that we were far enough away to be safe, we would hang the antenna and call in.

That great solution to our problem caused Ken to take the decision away from us and make it himself. He said, "You are being evacuated immediately by helicopter." In our state of mind, we hadn't seen what was so easy for everyone else to see. Gail and I, with all our stuff, just what the people wanted, would be sitting in the canoe with the Vakabuis paddlers, and Sahu and Yakub would be up the trees. All they would have to do would be to paddle off with us!

Personally, I was relieved when the decision was taken away from us, as I was feeling quite stressed making decisions that would reflect the feelings of all of us and that could determine if we lived or died. We asked that there be no police and no guns, so it was decided that Jim Harris would come in and take us out two at a time.

We didn't tell the people that we had heard them talking, but we told them that we were being called back to Senggo. We promised that we would return soon and for them not to run away. The helicopter arrived about 11:00 a.m. Gail and Yakub were evacuated on the first shuttle, and Sahu and I went out on the second one.

We were evacuated to Binam, where we spent the night. Dominggus Mayor came by outboard and arrived just before dark. Our shelter there was a hut with a palm frond roof and bark floor with no walls. I slept on the end and got the worse part of a heavy rain storm in the middle of the night. I was glad when the night was over. We left about 5:00 a.m. on Wednesday and arrived at Senggo about 9:30 a.m.

We may never know whether or not the Vakabuis people would have carried out the plans they were discussing, but we feel that the right decision was made. In retrospect, it looks very likely that they were indeed serious. Several things point to this. One was the fact that Sahu had been invited on

Sunday to go hunting on Tuesday with Dasawu. They could have easily killed him in the jungle, and that would have been consistent with their culture. The fact that the chief of Esaun, Boar, was involved on Sunday hints that he could have been encouraging something like this to obtain the items we had. Then the fact that they were so nice and cooperative after Sunday and seemingly anxious that we not return suddenly to Senggo also hinted that they were making some plans. Their culture of deceit and treachery all seem to indicate that they did have unpleasant plans for us.

Evacuation

We were very disappointed in this setback to the ministry to the Vakabuis and Esaun people. However, we continued to believe that God would build His church among those people for whom He died.

CHAPTER 8

Revival at Senggo

February 1983 – September 1985

T he day after we arrived at Senggo after having been evacuated, Sahu came to me and said, "Nona, just because they were going to kill us doesn't mean that we can forget them. We must go back." A couple of days later, some of the men, including Sahu, did go back for a couple of hours to reassure the people that we had not forsaken them.

During the next two and one-half years, we continued our ministry to the Vakabuis people. Various people, including myself, visited them, sharing more of God's Word with them and encouraging them. They continually asked for someone to live with them to teach them. We continued to pray that God would call a Senggo Christian family who would be willing to live with them.

During this time we were experiencing revival at Senggo. Several hundred people made professions of faith during a short period of time. The converts were trained, and hundreds were baptized. It was a joyous time for all of us!

However, no one was ready to live at Vakabuis on a more-or-less permanent basis, but Clarence did place a teacher from the Auyu tribe, Mihel Tagi, and his family with them. Mihel had the disadvantage of not knowing the Citak language. However, he learned to communicate some with them, and he, along with a Citak interpreter from Senggo, had a good ministry there. The people were understanding more and more, and we continued to pray and long for the day when God would begin to build His church there. Our dreams began to come true in September 1985.

Our First Vakabuis Convert

September 12–16, 1985

THURSDAY: Ruth Dougherty, Yos Ondi (the motorist from Sentani), Alfons Fiak (an evangelist from Senggo), and I went to Vakabuis by boat to spend several days. Vakabuis was in a state of confusion and disorderliness when we arrived. The river had overflowed from heavy rains and had branched off right through Mihel's house which was standing in about two and one-half feet of water that reached to just a few inches below the floor. The village, a few feet away, was very muddy but not completely flooded.

Pigs rooting in the mud made it worse. It took the men most of the afternoon to put up the poles for the radio antenna because of the water and the swift current. One of the poles was in water almost neck-deep.

Staying with Mihel was only slightly better than where we had stayed before. His house had two rooms with a cook house built on to it. The house was made in the usual Citak fashion by tying poles together for the frame, palm fronds for the roof, a bark floor, and palm stems for the walls—no furniture, of course. Mihel took Ruth and me into the bedroom and said that we could sleep wherever we wanted—on the bed with him and his wife or on the floor! The "bed" was just a raised platform. Great choice! We asked if we could sleep in the sitting/dining room expecting that Yos and Alfons would sleep in the bedroom with them. He agreed, so we put down our bedding and moved in.

Then we braved the water and waded over to the village to visit. When we returned, there were two sleeping mats on a raised platform next to my sleeping bag. That was when we realized that the four of us were sleeping together. That wouldn't have been so bad except that Alfons, who was right next to me, kept moaning, groaning, talking, slapping mosquitoes, and thrashing about in his sleep. It was probably from eating too much!

Each morning we would ask him how he had slept, and he always said, "Fine." We assured him that we hadn't!

To add to the sleeping difficulties, my air mattress sprang a leak. I had to get up and blow it up two or three times every night.

It is always very interesting to live in the village with no facilities, but it is even more interesting when the "non-facilities" are under two and one-half feet of water!

That first night for supper we had boiled fish, sago, and some sandwiches that we had brought.

■ ■ ■

FRIDAY: We had sago for breakfast. Fortunately, Ruth had brought her ever-present peanut butter and honey which did wonders for the sago.

We trudged through the water and mud again to visit. Everywhere we went, they would wash off our muddy feet after we had climbed the poles up into their houses. Sedo's wife appeared about ready to deliver a baby, and Ruth, a nurse, began asking questions about her children. We learned that she had had six children, with only one living. When Ruth asked about the other children, she laughingly told her that she had choked them to death when they were born because she didn't want them. Ruth talked to her and encouraged her not to kill the baby that was due to be born soon.

For lunch we had *pepeda,* boiled fish, and rice. *Pepeda* is "sago." I would rather eat sago grubs any day than *pepeda.* It is made by simply pouring boiling water over sago and turning it into a gluey, slimy mess that takes a lot of grace to eat. Both Ruth and I got it down—barely—and were pleased that it stayed down.

That night we showed a filmstrip, and Alfons gave an excellent message. Then we had supper of baked fish, sago, and squash.

■   ■   ■

SATURDAY: Breakfast was sago, peanut butter, and honey. Early that morning Ruth provided us with some entertainment by falling through the porch into the water with a bucket of water. We fished her out and dried her off, and she was all right.

We would talk with the people each day as they would come in and out throughout the day. We also visited each of the houses in the village every day. On Saturday morning Ruth decided to give a health lesson to a lady who had come to visit. She had 13 flashcards and had gotten through the third card when the lady said, "*Arura,*" ("Finished") and got up and left leaving Ruth looking a bit stunned! So much for the exciting health lesson!

There is never any doubt when they have had enough. They can turn you off, and there is no way you can get their attention again until they get good and ready to listen! They haven't learned to pretend to be interested like we Americans do!

Bidaw came that morning with an older man to visit. He said that the other man was from the village of Asarep and that he was his father. That didn't make sense to us as the Asarep people were their enemies, so I began to question him and learned this very interesting story.

Several years earlier, the older man had stolen a girl from Vakabuis. Then later some people friendly with the Asarep people had killed and eaten Bidaw's father. They had also killed his mother and had left her body to rot. In revenge, Bidaw had stolen the man who had stolen the Vakabuis girl. He brought him back to Vakabuis to replace his own father who had been killed and eaten. The man seemed quite happy to have been stolen and said, "Bidaw is my son." That sounds very strange from our way of thinking but completely understandable from theirs.

We had an earthquake that morning, and the cook house began making uncertain noises as Mihel ran out of it. The poles were old and rotten. Ruth and I were in the house but couldn't easily run out of it unless we wanted to swim. We learned later by listening to the other missionaries talking on the single sideband radio that the center of the quake was in the mountains north of us where landslides destroyed gardens and killed two people. Some missionaries were evacuated.

Lunch was nothing! Yos and Alfons had gone upriver to visit the village of Esaun, and I guess Mihel's wife figured that Ruth and I didn't need anything. By about 3:00 p.m., we decided to cook, so we baked fish and sago over the open fire.

That night we showed another film strip, and Alfons gave another good message.

Then we had supper which was leftover rice. That was all they served, saying there was no fish, meaning that there was no fresh fish in the net that afternoon. However, there were lots of fish on the smoking rack over the fire which had been caught earlier in OUR net. We asked for it. We were really hungry for fish.

That night Ruth went out on the "porch" to brush her teeth—in the dark! Don't try that unless you have toothpaste in a florescent tube. Ruth almost brushed her teeth with Pragmatar, an anti-fungus ointment!

■　■　■

SUNDAY: It had rained quite a bit the night before and was still raining when we got up. The water level had risen several more inches and was almost to the floor of the house. We reported to Senggo that morning, and Clarence, our station head, advised us to consider coming home that day instead of waiting until Monday as planned in case it kept raining and flooded us out. We decided to make the decision by noon.

For breakfast we had sago, peanut butter, and honey. The weather was so bad that I declared that if anyone wanted to see me that day that they would have to come to where I was because I had no intentions of getting out in that mess for anyone! I was all for canceling the service figuring nobody would come anyway. However, after some counsel and "encouragement" from Ruth, we packed up the cassette player, picture roll, jackets, cameras, and umbrellas, got in the boat and paddled across to the village. I was so glad later that we did.

There was a house that had just the poles, roof, and floor where we decided to have the service. A good group came. The house had a slick pole for "steps," and the first fellow to go up fell off in the mud. We said, "No way," but did manage somehow to get up in the house with some pushing and pulling from the people.

The people enjoyed the cassette, so we played the sto-

Kanma

ries of the death, burial, and resurrection of Christ, and then Alfons preached it using the picture roll. He ended with the story of the two roads—the narrow one to Heaven and the wide one to Hell. He talked about confession of sin. The people thought that they were supposed to confess to each other and thought it was hilarious! They began to talk and laugh, and Kanma began confessing to stealing someone's fish line! We all got involved in trying to explain to them, and it turned into a "service" such as you have never seen.

Service

Finally Alfons asked them if anyone wanted to confess his sins to God, and Kanma said, "I do."

Utan immediately said, "Me too." Utan was the one who had sat on my lap the first time we went into the village.

After the service, we invited Kanma and Utan to come to the house with us. What a thrill it was to watch the Holy Spirit open their hearts and minds to understand the Gospel and their need of forgiveness! What a thrilling experience it was to hear them pray for the first time as they confessed their sins to God and asked for forgiveness! They were the first people from Vakabuis to enter the family of God—just five years from that first visit to their village. I was so excited to realize, "These two headhunter cannibals are my brothers!"

Kanma and Utan—first converts!

We were really concerned for Bidaw. He had always seemed to be more receptive and interested than anyone else in the village. He seemed to have a depth of understanding that no one else had. He had sat in deep thought throughout the service that morning but didn't make any move. I was so disappointed. Feeling that perhaps we would have another opportunity to talk with him later, we felt that we should stay that night. We reported this decision to Clarence at noon.

Then we were disappointed to learn later that Bidaw had gone pig hunting and didn't plan to return to the village until the next day. This of course meant that we would not have another opportunity to talk with him as we would need to leave early in the morning.

We had a real Christmas-like dinner of rice, canned corned beef, and dried peas but no sago, no fish, and NO rat.

That evening Yos brought some of the women with babies over in the boat, and other women, along with the men, came in canoes or waded through the water for the film strip and message by Alfons.

After everyone had gone home and we were preparing to eat (sago and baked fish), Bidaw showed up. He said that he didn't see any pigs, so he came home. He did bring a large fish, which he gave me. I was standing on the porch with him, and he said, "Nona, I killed and ate people. I split an Asarep man's chest open with an ax and killed him. I stole girls from Esaun."

At first I didn't know what he was doing, and then I realized that he was confessing his sin! I invited him in. Ruth,

Alfons and Bidaw

Alfons, and I talked with him for quite a while. He said that Mihel had been talking with him and that he had heard about the narrow path to Heaven and the wide path to Hell and that he had been thinking about it for a long time. He said that he wanted to be on the path to Heaven.

He asked, "When I killed and ate those people, God saw me, didn't He?"

"Yes, Bidaw," I said, "God saw you, but that is why we came here—to tell you that He loves you and can forgive you."

He seemed genuinely convicted by his sin, and it was a joy to hear him pray for the first time in his life! He said, "God, I have killed and eaten people. I split that Asarep man's chest open with an ax. I have stolen women from Esaun. God, just don't think about that any more." That is their way of asking for forgiveness, and I was thinking, "God has forgotten and will never remember them again!" I have never experienced any greater joy when I remembered the indescribable honor and privilege of seeing Bidaw enter the family of God. I had another cannibal brother.

God had begun to build His church at Vakabuis.

■　■　■

MONDAY: We had sago, peanut butter, and honey for breakfast. We loaded our things in the boat in the rain. When we pushed off to leave, the cook house collapsed into the water.

Pictured right: The cook house collapsed into the water!

From Cannibalism to Christianity

We traveled in a hard rain all the way to Binam, which made it a miserable trip, except for the joy we were experiencing because of the first converts at Vakabuis.

We ate lunch at Binam—cassowary bird! I felt like shouting! The "bird" was tough as leather, but it was a welcome change from what we had been eating.

We arrived back at Senggo thrilled at what God was doing in Vakabuis and that Kanma, Utan, and Bidaw were now a part of God's family. Still, we were very concerned for others. We were praying for Pau, the chief, who had never yet showed a lot of interest in the Gospel. Also, we were praying for Sedo, who was always so friendly with us and seemed happy to see us, but like his chief, not really interested in the Gospel. We were concerned for the women who were still very shy and not very talkative with us.

Shortly after that, Mihel's wife died rather suddenly, leaving four small children. The result of her sudden passing was Mihel's not being able to return to Vakabuis.

We continued to pray that God would lead some Senggo family to go there and live with the Vakabuis people and to teach them God's Word in their own language.

We didn't know that God was already dealing with Silas Senggo and his wife, Marta.

CHAPTER

10

A Need Filled

September 1985 — April 1986

We felt that it was imperative that a Citak-speaking evangelist be placed at Vakabuis. However, no one who qualified was willing to live with them on a permanent basis. We continued to pray that the Lord would speak to the one He had chosen for this task.

Silas and Marta Senggo are a Christian couple from Senggo. They had not been on our minds at all as candidates for this ministry. However, one day Silas came to me and said, "Nona, I don't want to be saved and then just sit around. I want to do something for the Lord." We talked to him about a possible assignment in Vakabuis, and he seemed thrilled with the prospect.

Silas went up and built a small "house" which was just poles in the ground with palm fronds as the walls and roof. That quickly built house became the first "parsonage" at Vakabuis.

In April 1986, I had the joy of going along to introduce the first Citak lady from Senggo to the Vakabuis people. Marta had been showing some real apprehension, and I had been spending time encouraging her and assuring her that I would not leave her there unless I was sure she would be safe.

The big day arrived, and Marta, looking very fearful, got into the boat with her two small children. I assured her again that the Vakabuis people would receive her well. Then Yos Ondi started the motor, and we started out. I looked across at Marta, and she was holding on for dear life! Her eyes were as big as saucers, and it was then that I realized that she wasn't afraid of the Vakabuis people at all—she was terrified of that boat ride! She had never traveled any faster than a canoe in her life! We laughed, and she cried, and then we comforted her! Quite soon she got over her fear and enjoyed the rest of the trip.

We arrived to see the lovely "parsonage" standing in a couple of feet of water, so again we "enjoyed" the inconvenience of either wading in the water or riding in a canoe around the village. Setting up housekeeping was really fun! On second thought, the word "fun" doesn't really describe it! The house wasn't completed, so some of the men were putting up the rest of the palm fronds on the roof. Marta jokingly ridiculed them as they worked. She made a hit with the people right from the beginning.

Sedo

Bidaw made several dives into the water to get mud to put on the floor of the house to make a place for us to build our cook fire.

The BIG job, insisted on by Marta and me, was to build a small room on to the house for our "bathroom." It also was just poles in the ground with palm fronds around it and, of course, they had to build it in the water.

While we were setting up the house, Sedo yelled across from his house, "*Uruda auaba!*" ("Ruth is here.") *Uruda* is the way they pronounce "Ruth."

Thinking that he was asking if Ruth had come with us, I yelled back, "No, Ruth didn't come."

He repeated a bit louder, "*Uruda auaba!*"

I yelled back a bit louder, "No, Ruth didn't come."

After repeating this exchange several times, Sedo finally turned around, picked up a cute baby girl with a big bushy head of hair, held her up, and yelled, "*Uruda auaba, Uruda auaba.*" His wife had given birth to the baby; and since Ruth had encouraged her not to kill the baby, they had named the baby after her!

Pau was very friendly and help-ful this trip. He attended the serv-ices and really liked Silas. For the first time, he showed a gen-uine interest in the Gospel.

We stayed with Silas and Marta for several days, and it was such a joy to see how the Vakabuis people accepted them. Some of them would come to me and say, "Is he going to stay here and teach us?" The day we were to leave, several came

Uruda

From Cannibalism to Christianity

Silas preaching

and said, "When you leave, don't you take Silas with you. Leave him here."

As we were leaving, I looked back, and Silas, Marta, and their two small children were standing in their doorway. Their "house" was filled to capacity with the Vakabuis people. I was so thrilled that God had led them to serve Him in that very difficult place, but as usual, Satan had other plans.

Silas, Marta, and children

God's Church Continues to Grow

April 1986 – September 1986

S ilas and Marta had been at Vakabuis only a few days when Marta had a serious gall bladder attack, and they had to return to Senggo. Silas returned alone to work on a better house for them, and then they returned together. However, Marta suffered from an attack of malaria along with her gall bladder problem and had to return to Senggo yet again.

These problems continually reminded us that invading Satan's territory cannot be done without casualties. We continued to pray for Silas and Marta and for the Vakabuis people.

In September 1986, Ruth, along with some summer workers, went up just for a day, but what an exciting trip! The following is what happened in Ruth's words:

■ ■ ■

"When we arrived, a young mother, naked and covered with mud [a sign of mourning], was sitting up on a rack by her home, grieving over the dead body of her preschool-age son. Although the little body was wrapped in leaves, the people claimed he had been dead for five days. The flies and stench verified this, but our attempts to persuade them to bury the child proved to be futile. What sorrow for these who have no hope!

Noak gathered the people together and shared the story of the ten lepers with them. At the close of the service, three young men named Ndoak, Zuam, and Tupun professed to accept Christ as Saviour and Lord. Thrilling!"

■ ■ ■

God's church in Vakabuis now numbered six!

12

First Church Building

September 1986 – April 1987

Noak continued to be a blessing, and we placed him in one of the Brazza area villages. The village had no Christians and was steeped in darkness such as most people would never understand.

The Citak people fear black magic, and if they feel that a curse has been put on them, they do not resist thinking that it would be useless. Noak felt that someone in that village put a curse on him, and the spirits revealed to him that he would drown. Noak did something no other Citak person had ever done to our knowledge. He resisted. One day while fishing, his fish hook got caught on a log on the bottom of the river. Normally, the person would just jump in and drown because of the curse. However, Noak prayed, dived in, and rescued his fish hook. I was so very proud of him!

However, that started a process in Noak's life where he was convinced that a curse had been put on him. He eventually blamed—not the villagers there—but a Christian man from the Indonesian language church at Senggo. Noak was showing signs of serious paranoia. We were praying.

Silas continued to make trips to Vakabuis alone, staying a few days at a time. Marta continued to have serious health problems. We continued to pray.

Around the end of 1986, they were finally able to return

and stay. Silas had built a better house and in a nicer place where it wouldn't flood during the rainy season.

Gail and I went up in April 1987. Marta's health had improved, and they seemed happy at Vakabuis. The people were very pleased with them. What a joy it was to know that they were there teaching the people on a regular basis!

The highlight of that trip was to see their first church "building" going up! When we arrived, the people were really excited and kept pulling me along to show me something. Some explanations are needed here. This "building" consisted of poles in the ground with palm fronds on the roof—no walls. The "pews" were logs on the ground. It wasn't even nice enough to be called a brush arbor, but to me it was as beautiful as any impressive edifice I had ever seen. I took so many pictures of it, you would have thought it was a mansion!

First church building

CHAPTER 13

A New Work
at Bubis/Esaun

April 1987 – September 1989

O n a one-day trip to Vakabuis, I noticed that it was
very apparent that Bidaw's wife was going to have a
baby at any time. It was also apparent that she was
probably going to have twins. They believed that if a woman
gave birth to twins, one was the child of an evil spirit. The
husband usually beat his wife, and they killed one of the twins.
I was afraid to talk to them or suggest that she might have
twins, for fear of frightening them, especially since it was possible that she really would not have twins.

A couple of weeks later, Ruth
went up for a visit and found two
beautiful baby girls—Daomi and
Dina—the first twins to survive
at Vakabuis. Bidaw said very
proudly, "We didn't kill them!"

On one trip we learned the
following information. Sedo, who
always seemed so friendly and
was seldom seen without a big
smile, was there. He had had five
wives, but two had run away to

Twins Daomi and Dina

another village some time ago because they were afraid of him. A few weeks before our visit, another wife had run away to another man in the village and said that she wanted to be his wife. That man was Dasawo—the man who wanted to steal Gail and me.

Sedo was angry and had chased her into the jungle, killed her, and left the body where she had died. Several days later another wife died. The people said that Sedo had done black magic on her. Now he was down to one wife. Sedo had not trusted Christ.

Also on that trip Bidaw told us that his baby was very sick with diarrhea and that he and Silas had prayed for it, and the baby got all better.

Then one day word came to Senggo that Sedo had died. We were so disappointed to get that word. He had always been friendly to us and was always glad to see us when we came to Vakabuis. He was not involved in the uprising against us when Gail and I were evacuated. However, Sedo did not appear to be interested in the Gospel. It was disappointing to know that one of these people whom we had grown to love was not rescued from the clutches of Satan and died without knowing Christ as his Saviour.

During all this time, we had not forgotten the people in the other Brazza villages. How we longed for enough Citak-speaking Christians to place some in each of these villages. For some of them, we had to depend on periodic visits from a variety of people, including missionaries as well as nationals, to teach them as much as we could.

Bubis/Esaun

Tamnim is a village located just about five minutes' walk from Senggo. Oto and Paulina Arenu are from that village. They were led to serve the Lord in the village of Bubis and had been there for several years teaching the people there. The village of Esaun recently moved and joined the village of Bubis. We were happy about that since they now also have regular teaching from Oto.

For several months, Oto had been asking me to come to the village of Bubis/Esaun to teach the people about how to receive the Lord as their Saviour. Although he had taught them well, he was still a bit unclear as to how to go about actually bringing them to the Lord.

Dominggus took Gail and me up with the boat, and we stayed for three days in September 1989. The village was depressing. It was wet and VERY muddy. We walked in mud everywhere we went.

When we arrived, a young girl who had given birth to a baby girl a couple of days before was about to kill her on orders from her husband. She had given birth to the baby under the house in ankle-deep mud. Neither she nor the baby had been allowed in the house, but they had built a small lean-to on to the back of the house for them. They were both indescribably filthy. The baby already had several infections although she was just a couple of days old.

They regularly kill baby girls in some of those villages, so we talked quite sternly to the husband and made a few threats and "convinced" them not to kill the baby. We also got the wife to clean up herself and to bathe the baby, and Gail treated the infections.

We had a service that evening in the front of the village. People were sitting on pieces of wood, etc., in the mud. Oto preached. The only house large enough to accommodate all the people in the village would have been the bachelor house, and it was in terrible shape. It didn't have any walls, and the poles were rotting. We feared that, if we all got in it, we would all be on the ground!

I was feeling a bit discouraged. Their language is a different dialect, so I was having trouble understanding them, although they seemed to understand me. Also, their thoughts were on a man who was missing. He had gone to Senggo with some other people but had left without them several days before they did. He had never showed up at Bubis/Esaun. They were convinced that the people in the village of Jinak had killed him, and they were mourning for him. Some were discussing making a raid on the village of Jinak. He turned up several days later and had been out in the swamp hunting for crocodiles!

The next morning we had a service in the yard, and then Gail held a Mother-Baby Clinic. She had expected to weigh about six to eight babies, but she weighed about thirty! Also, several from the village of Serai just down river came up.

While she was doing that, I sat in the yard with the women as they waited their turn. It was wild. They were all over me, and several little girls wanted to sit on my lap. They tried to find lice on my head, and just about all of them wanted to see for themselves that I didn't have any—unheard of! Then one lady screamed that she had found a louse "egg," and everyone had to see for themselves. I'm SURE it was just a speck of dirt!

Then someone discovered my dental partial! I had about a dozen very dirty fingers in my mouth, and it was really funny watching their expressions when I took it out! They would call for others to come and see, and I had to take it out about a dozen times! That evening I had to do it all over again for the men!

In the afternoon we visited in the houses and talked with the people. We had a good talk with Boar, the Esaun chief, who was one of the main agitators against Gail and me when we were evacuated from Vakabuis. He had become chief after having killed and helped to eat three people. We talked about the death of Sedo. Boar said, "He went to Hell, didn't he?"

On Sunday morning it was raining, so we decided to take a chance and have the service inside the bachelor house. We climbed into it very carefully and almost cleared out a couple of times when it made some threatening creaks, but it stood. Oto preached a good sermon. After the service, five men came saying that they wanted to be saved. Among them was Boar.

What a special thrill it was to have the privilege of leading him to the Lord! Afterward I asked him, "Boar, who is your Father now?"

He answered, "God."

"He is also my Father," I said. "So what does that make us?"

He said with a smile, "We are brother and sister." Boar, who at one time wanted to kill us, was

Boar

now our brother, and God had begun to build His church at Bubis\Esaun.

CHAPTER 14

God Speaks Citak

1990 – 1995

Ruth and Abdon made a visit to Vakabuis and had the joyful privilege of leading the first Vakabuis women to the Lord. One of them was Daso, Utan's wife.

In August 1992, several war chiefs from Esaun came to Senggo for a visit. They asked the Senggo church leaders to allow them to do something in the Sunday morning service. This came as a complete surprise to me. They came dressed up in their war paint and feathers, wielding their weapons. They ran back and forth on the platform pretending that they were going to war.

Then they stopped and gave a wonderful testimony about how the Gospel had come to their village and how they had given up fighting and killing and were now trusting the Lord and following Him. As a token of their commitment, one of them came off the platform and presented his bow and arrows to me. I treasure this gift.

My prayer letter to friends and supporters in October 1995

Presenting their weapons

had this large title, "GOD SPEAKS CITAK." The most exciting experience of my missionary career was the Vakabuis experience. The most rewarding experience was the joy and privilege of translating the New Testament into the Citak language. The testament was dedicated in October 1995, and what a day that was for us!

Government officials and missionaries from other parts of the island were in attendance, along with guests from the United States. They included our General Director and wife, Dr. and Mrs. Richard Winchell; my missionary brother Stan, his wife Jane, and their daughter Tamah; and a supporting pastor and wife, Mr. and Mrs. Janice Turner.

We took them up by outboard motor to visit Vakabuis.

Margaret, Stan Stringer, Bidaw, Dr. Winchell

I translated the "Jesus" film into Citak, and we went to Vakabuis to show it on one trip. We had an old-fashioned filmstrip projector which was powered by a car battery. We hung a sheet in the middle of the village while the people sat on the ground. It was fun sitting among the people to hear their reaction.

They kept a running commentary about what they were seeing and gave expressions of sympathy when Jesus was arrested, beaten, and killed. When Jesus told His disciples that He would rise again, the people said, "He said He would rise from the dead!"

Some of the men from Senggo had an exciting experience on another trip there. They were having a service in the yard when Pau began to wave his hands in the middle of the sermon. He indicated that he wanted to confess his sins to God. Abdon asked him to wait until he finished his sermon, but Pau didn't want to wait. So they stopped the service and led him to the Lord. I was so sorry that I missed that exciting day.

When the picture of Jesus after the resurrection came up on the screen, one man excitedly exclaimed, "He DID rise again. LOOK, there He is!"

The Christians at Vakabuis were growing in number and in their knowledge of God's Word; however, back at Senggo, some things were not going so well.

Pau and Margaret

CHAPTER

15

Noak

Noak continued to deteriorate and eventually became psychotic. The man from the Indonesian language church who was being blamed by Noak for having put a curse on him was from the island of Biak off the northwest coast of the island. There were several Biak families at Senggo who were all in the Indonesian language church. Noak became extremely paranoid and developed a deep hatred of all Biak people.

He felt that if he killed one of them, then the curse would be lifted off him. One day in late 1992, Mr. Yensenem, a Biak man, was visiting in the village when Noak sneaked up behind him with a hatchet. He jumped out suddenly and split Mr. Yensenem's head open. The hatchet went through his skull and into his brain.

Noak was not necessarily angry with Yensenem; his only fault was that he was a Biakker. This unwarranted attack set off many angry reactions and threats of retaliation towards Noak's relatives, mainly Titus Fiak, my main translation helper and Citak pastor, and Abdon Fiak. Titus' wife was Noak's sister. This situation threatened to become an all-out war between the Indonesian language church and the Citak language church as their old culture of revenge reappeared.

The translation ministry almost came to a halt as my primary helpers were in hiding. Other church activities either stopped or were poorly attended as the people were afraid. Several confrontations almost ended in bloodshed. One time the Citak people even got their spears and bows and arrows and prepared to go to war until someone said, "We have left that, and we are following the Lord!" They put down their weapons. Needless to say, this was a very difficult time for all of us.

Yensenem was in a coma for several weeks while his fellow Biakkers waited for him to regain consciousness and tell them what to do. It was a very tense time as Yensenem's two sons were very angry and making serious threats. As a result, many of the Fiak clan stayed hidden in the jungle. When he finally regained consciousness, the first thing he said was for them not to retaliate. His attitude has been great as he demonstrates the presence of God in his heart and life. He remains paralyzed on one side from the injury to his brain.

Our hearts grieved for both Yensenem and Noak. Noak was arrested and locked in a windowless room there at Senggo. Ruth and I visited him and hoped to see some sign of remorse. Remembering how he had wanted to be perfect for God, we asked him what he thought about all day in that room. He said, "I think about how hot it is in that room with no windows." Sad to say, he shows no sign of remorse.

They sent him out to the capitol to the very inefficient psychiatric hospital. When they brought him to the airstrip to leave Senggo, he looked so pitiful walking along in handcuffs looking a bit frightened but also a bit proud. The Senggo people mourned, and I mourned with them in my heart.

Eventually, apologies were made between Yensenem and Titus and Abdon, and relations between the churches began to return to normal.

However, Noak continued to deteriorate and became more determined in his efforts to kill a Biak person. He was eventually returned to Senggo, and he terrorized everyone there. He began directing his anger not only at the Biak people but also toward his own people.

One night while carrying his weapons—spear and knife, he began stalking the house of a Biak family. A young man from the Asmat tribe who had come to Senggo for medicine didn't know the situation with Noak and decided to be a hero and hold Noak. All the people were afraid to come out of their houses, and the young man was found dead the next morning.

Noak is still at Senggo, and there have been frequent incidents where he has threatened someone else. We have to have police guarding when we have a special service at night for the Indonesian congregation. His weapons have all been confiscated, and his wife is staying in another house out of fear for her own life.

Saying goodbye to Noak

Noak doesn't want to hear the name of God and becomes angry if it is mentioned. I left Senggo in October 2004, and the photo on page 117 shows my final goodbyes to him.

In the 40+ years I spent in Irian Jaya/Papua, this was no doubt my most disappointing experience. I loved Noak, and still do. I continue to claim him for the Lord. Satan has obviously won a battle, but I believe that God will win that war in the end.

CHAPTER

16

Out of the Darkness

1996–2005

In January 1999, a supporting pastor's wife, Mrs. Marcie Aiken, came for a visit, and what a time we had. We spent an exciting night at Vakabuis. Mihel was there, so we stayed with them in their hut, sleeping on the floor, and eating all sorts of "goodies." We ate one meal with a chicken trying to lay an egg on a shelf over the table!

On that trip I was told that Pau was serving the Lord and that Bidaw was the most faithful Christian in the village. We were saddened to learn that Utan had gone to "God's Village" several weeks earlier.

The people had stopped killing twins, but they continued to place their dead on racks in the yard. On one trip five decaying corpses were in the village, and almost everyone was sick. The smell was overpowering, so we didn't stay.

We kept encouraging them to bury their dead. One day Abdon was preaching out in the middle of the village and said, "God made us from dirt; and when we die, we return to dirt, so you should put the corpses in the ground."

I was standing at the back of the crowd, and one man lifted a very dirty arm to his nose, smelled it, and declared, "He is right. It IS dirt."

Eventually they did begin to bury their dead.

I was preparing to return to the United States to retire

after 40+ wonderful years in Papua. I made my final visit to Vakabuis. I asked Pau, "Are you following the Lord?"

"Yes," he said. "Whatever the preacher says to do, I am doing it." I assured him that I would meet him in God's Village.

I often talked to them about what God's Village was like; and when I did, I always felt that I sure would like to know what was going on in their minds. I thought about how nice it would be to get to Heaven first and see the looks on their faces when they enter that wonderful place. Their word for *amazement* is "to stand with your mouth open." I could just imagine their mouths open as wide as possible.

In August 2004, just two months before I left the field, word came that Bidaw was sick. Then several days later we learned that he had gone to God's Village. We mourned him, but I couldn't be too sad because I kept imagining what his mouth must look like. Then I thought, "Well, I guess now he will be standing there waiting to see my mouth when I enter." What a day that will be!

The people in the three villages told about in this book—Vakabuis, Esaun, and Serai—all asked us to help them build "permanent" church buildings. Two of them, Esaun and Serai, were built and dedicated just days before my departure.

How exciting it was to stand in front of the congregation at Esaun and see Boar sitting right up front. He was the chief who was involved in the uprising against us. Later he became a Christian. Following the service, he came to me outside and said, "The first time you came here, I was naked."

I said, "I know. You were also killing and eating people."

"Nona," he replied, "thank you for coming. Thank you for telling us how to go to God's Village. You brought us out of darkness into the light." I won't even attempt to describe how I felt.

Above: New church building at Serai
Below: New church building at Bubis/Esaun

Boar and me

Shortly after I arrived in the United States, word came that Pau also had gone to God's Village. Isn't it great knowing that there are former headhunter/cannibals in Heaven?

We have emphasized the story of Vakabuis, but this is just a small part of the real story of what God is doing in the Brazza River area, as well as in the entire Citak tribe. All of us who have served in the Citak tribe are praising God for the indescribable privilege of working together with Him and with each other to build His church in this area. I personally can think of nothing else that I would rather do with my life than to be partners with God in building His church in the Citak tribe. There is no greater blessing than to see the light of the glorious Gospel shine in their hearts, convict them of sin, and bring them to saving faith. What an honor!

God is building His church; and one day when we stand before Him, we will stand with Bidaw, Boar, Kanma, Utan,

Pau, and others from this area. They will stand before Him faultless and robed in white, and will hear Him say, "Welcome to My Village." What a day that will be!